SUCCESS W [D1584273]

Rachel Nelson *has* made it to the top – by her own
unaided efforts – in a PR consultancy and in executive
and senior management posts with Thames TV and
EMI. She is now a full-time writer.

Any woman with her eye on the boss's chair would do
well to invest in Rachel Nelson's excellent and amusing reference book. It is pithily written and fun to read.
Nottingham Evening Post

Rachel Nelson has written a book for women – that
every man should rush out and buy.
Brighton Argus

Tremendously readable, witty and amusing, yet full of
sound common sense.
West Sussex County Times

A route map to help an intelligent woman survive in
the office jungle.
Oxford Mail

SUCCESS WITHOUT TEARS

A Woman's Guide to the Top

Rachel Nelson

A STAR BOOK

published by
the Paperback Division of
W. H. ALLEN & Co. Ltd

A Star Book
Published in 1980
by the Paperback Division of
W. H. Allen & Co. Ltd
A Howard and Wyndham Company
44 Hill Street, London W1X 8LB

First published in Great Britain by
Weidenfeld & Nicolson

Copyright © Rachel Nelson 1979

Printed in Great Britain by
C. Nicholls & Company Ltd, The Philips Park Press, Manchester

ISBN 0 352 30653 X

*To all my ex-bosses, without whom
this book would not have been possible
(or necessary!)*

Contents

Preface

Intelligent women of all ages realize that there is a future for them in the business world. Many of them are already making it in industry and showing that they are just as capable of taking decisions and acting responsibly as their male colleagues.

For years male-dominated organizations have held women at bay, but even the most diehard male chauvinists are starting to realize that too many female brains are going to waste in the typing pool when they could be better employed in the board room.

If you are an intelligent woman with ambitions to get into management, whether you are starting at the bottom as a secretary or beginning higher up the ladder, with a degree, as a qualified solicitor, accountant or engineer, this book is a practical field guide which will help you to chart your path through the minefields and pitfalls which lie in wait for a female in this strange masculine world with all its rules and taboos, its primitive rituals, its prejudices and illogicalities.

This book will not tell you how to cope with your love-life outside the office, your domestic difficulties or your problems in combining a career and a family. It won't give you any qualifications, but it will help you to use the ones you've got. Look on it more as an AA book or a highway code which will help you to read the signs and signals on your journey through this fascinating territory, and to avoid accidents and confrontations.

Whatever business you are in, and whatever your role in that business, you will find the tips in this book applicable. The people and situations it describes are relevant and universal wherever large companies and organizations are found.

If you keep your head, your sense of proportion and your sense of humour, you will find your trip through the office jungle at worst an interesting intellectual exercise, at best, a rewarding experience. You may even become a member of that rarest of species, an executive director of the feminine gender.

If your fantasies tend to be less about walking up the aisle or baking the perfect cake, and more about sitting in the back of a limo reading the *Financial Times*, this book is for you.

I
Getting Started

> Mighty things from small beginnings grow.
> *John Dryden (1631–1700)*

There are many ways in which a woman can start a career, but most women still begin as secretaries. It is fashionable nowadays to run down shorthand and typing as a starting point. The argument is that once you are labelled as a secretary you will never become anything else.

I find this argument unconvincing.

Armed with secretarial skill, a woman of almost any age has an unequalled choice and mobility. A good secretary can pick and choose not only her company, but the industry or – if she is a free agent – the part of the world where she wants to work. If she is ambitious, she can shop around for the job where her chances of promotion look the most promising. The anti-short-hand-and-typing lobby underestimates women by assuming that once a woman has become a secretary, she won't have the guts either to break out of the mould and get herself promoted, or move to another company where her talents are more likely to get the recognition they deserve.

The secret is not to let yourself get bogged down. Be flexible.

Lack of confidence, a problem which bedevils the vast majority of the female sex, is the main drawback for older women.

After years of domestic life in their own homes, women feel they are simply not up to plunging into the tough business world outside. Even women who held quite important positions before they got married and became 'housewives' suffer this feeling of inferiority. They feel they have become dull and housebound and unable to cope with modern office life. Or they

3

feel they may be laughed at by their families or the younger generation of office workers.

I can assure you that this feeling of inadequacy will soon wear off once you have taken the plunge. The thing is to get started. Once the initial shock has worn off and you have learnt to adapt to your surroundings you will soon feel at ease with your fellow students or workers. Women now make up over 40 per cent of the British labour force, so you won't be alone.

If you do your job properly and start by keeping a low profile, you will find yourself quickly accepted and respected, both while training and later in your chosen occupation.

Younger women need have no qualms. They belong to a generation which expects women to have jobs and be given equal opportunities with men. That the latter is still more fancy than fact is proved by the statistics at the end of this book, but at least the idea is now accepted and has even been approved by Parliament. A younger woman's only difficulty may come when she gets married and finds that she has to choose between a husband and children and a career. If you have that sort of husband then you have got a problem. But it is one outside the scope of this book, which is purely a guide to business life and how to progress within it.

But let's start at the beginning.

Here you are, an intelligent and ambitious woman, determined to get on in the great male-dominated world of industry and big business. Even if you are not ambitious, why not give it a try? Leigh-Mallory climbed Everest 'because it was there'. So are these large companies. Their challenge is equally provocative.

Whether you're a teenager straight out of school, or a middle-aged lady whose children are growing up, or a getting-on-for-sixty granny, my advice is the same. Enrol yourself in a short-hand/audio typing course. It needn't cost very much. Your local authority runs lessons for school leavers, adult education courses, retraining schemes for older people. Don't be put off by the idea of going back to school at your age. More and more people are doing it. If you are older it may take a bit longer, but get yourself up to a speed of at least 100 in shorthand and 50 in typing. You will then be better qualified than most of the so-called secretaries around. If you can also spell and take down a telephone message correctly you will be a pearl beyond price.

Dim-witted dolly-bird secretaries as status symbols are beginning to look as old-fashioned and tatty as some of the discredited wheeler-dealers who used to employ them, and survive mainly in film and TV comedies.

At long last reliability and efficiency seem to be coming back into fashion, and secretaries are no longer chosen purely for the shape of their legs.

Having taken your exams and obtained your certificates, you have passed the first hurdle and the world is your oyster. Go to a secretarial agency and you will probably be amazed by the warmth of your welcome. Sign on as a 'temp' and be prepared to go wherever they send you – it's all good experience. You will find that even in these hard times, there is a wide variety of jobs to choose from, particularly in the summer, when people are on holiday, and in the depths of winter when everyone's got flu.

Being a temp not only gives you a chance to gain experience and get paid for it. You can do it as and when you feel like it and it gives you the chance to shop around and get the feel of all sorts of different offices and a wide range of companies, businesses and government departments.

Do you fancy a bureaucratic atmosphere or something a bit livelier? Now is the time to find out.

Your agency is making money out of you, so if you don't feel you're getting the most interesting assignments, don't be afraid to ask for a change of scene. Just because you've done two stints with lawyers or stockbrokers, there is no reason to get type-cast. Ask for something different next time. There are plenty of agencies around and yours won't want to lose you, especially if you're doing a good job.

If you are doing your job conscientiously and responsibly and showing that you have initiative, you will sooner or later be approached and asked if you would like to stay on as a permanent member of the staff.

This is the danger point.

No matter how much at home you feel in this particular

office or how congenial you find the atmosphere, ask yourself two questions. Is this just a cosy cul-de-sac? What, if any, are your chances of promotion?

However strong the temptation, don't stay in any job where there is obviously no future for you outside your typewriter. Firms of architects, lawyers, patent, insurance or estate agents, accountants or any other organization where getting to the top depends on having a professional or technical qualification are not for you, so don't waste your time there.

Regretfully but firmly you must leave and move on. Advertising, television, the fashion business, journalism, public relations, are all fields in which prejudice against women is less severe. And, strangely enough, some of the areas like heavy industry which appear forbiddingly masculine are sometimes fertile ground for a female with ambition. But just a word of warning: look out for union problems. If you have ambitions in journalism for instance, there are certain magazines and newspapers where you are forbidden to move from a secretarial job to a journalistic one, and where articles are not accepted unless they are written by members of the National Union of Journalists. So always make enquiries early on.

Here are some suggestions.

Advertising

Good copy-writers are like gold and if you can develop the knack you can become one of the real money-spinners. It's worth having a try in an advertising agency, to see what makes the business tick. You may be one of the lucky ones who is genuinely creative and has a flair for selling a product in the press or on TV. One of the qualifications you need is a fertile mind and the skill to put your ideas across.

Women are often very successful in advertising, for example the legendary Mary Wells, who first hit the headlines when she decided to paint the entire fleet of an American airline in pastel colours. It was a gimmick, but nobody else had thought of it and it worked. If you have any talents in this direction the only way to find out is to get a secretarial job and sniff the atmosphere. If you feel at home in it stay around for a bit and watch your chance.

Television

The days when a secretary was thrown a stop-watch and told to get into the studio and direct a programme, because there wasn't anybody else around to do it, are alas over. They must have been stirring times and there are a number of female producers and directors around to this day to prove it.

Things are a lot tougher now, with a lot of programme makers out of work and with younger ones trying to get in. The slump in the film industry hasn't helped either, with redundant film directors looking for work. However you have got the advantage of them. You may know nothing about directing but you are a qualified secretary, and TV like any other industry has to get its letters typed and in this case its scripts as well. Having got yourself in, it is possible to become a research or a production assistant if you are in the right place at the right time. Here again you have to watch for the union problem. It is different in the BBC and ITV.

It's up to you to make yourself indispensable – then after that, who knows? Like all creative industries it's short of talent. If you've got it, you're in the right place to get noticed.

Fashion

The rag trade has always been a happy hunting ground for bright females. I suppose the top of the tree is to become a designer, but that usually means an art school training. Aim more at the business and selling side of things. If you've got the right approach and are good at getting on with people you could become a vendeuse in a fashion house. The big couture establishments have been feeling the pinch lately, but there are always a few very rich women who can afford these clothes. The really top fashion houses are very few and far between unless you go abroad, so it's probably better to aim lower down, at the ready-to-wear market where wheeling and dealing is intense but highly enjoyable if you thrive in that sort of atmosphere. If you've got a fashion flair it's worth trying your luck at a big store. Eventually you could get the chance to take a training course and, if you've got it right, you could become a buyer, a highly valued and powerful member of the hierarchy.

Journalism

I have already mentioned journalism as a career for women, but things in Fleet Street are very bad just now, with papers threatened with closure and freelances having a thin time. Provincial papers are in a healthier state and you may find that starting off as a secretary on a local paper may give you a toe-hold. It will certainly be interesting if nothing else. Unions are not always such a stumbling block in the provinces or in magazines, and you can start to try your hand at writing yourself once you've seen the kind of thing that's wanted. Certain magazines, like *She* for instance, do not at the present time insist on NUJ membership for their writers. They will print anything if they think it is good. Once you have had an article printed, joining the union becomes easier.

If it's power you're after and you've got your sights on the editor's chair, a woman's magazine is probably the best place to start your career.

Selling

Many women spend their lives selling themselves to men, so selling should be a tailor-made job for ambitious females. For some reason, perhaps the travelling involved, there arc very few salesladies 'on the road'. There are stay-at-home sales jobs, though, like Tupperware and Avon, which can lead to an important position, perhaps as area sales manager.

Public Relations

If tact and diplomacy and an eye for publicity are your strong points, it is well worth getting a job in a PR firm of consultants. There are a number to be found in any large town, though the big ones – mostly American – are usually based in London, in some cases with branches all over the world. An intelligent woman has a particularly good chance in the world of PR because it is not a profession which attracts top male talent. The last thing a smart young man straight out of university or business school thinks of going into is PR. It's way down the list of his priorities – partly because PR has a slightly seedy reputation, and partly because there doesn't seem to be much money in it. This is a mistake: there is lots of money to be made in PR if you are successful, and there are PR companies with very good reputations. Where America leads, the UK tends to follow, and it is possible to make a very good living.

It is best to start in a consultancy, as they will have a diversity of different 'accounts'. This will give you experience in promoting all sorts of products. If you are the right material you will soon be given a chance and there are no serious union problems to worry about.

Once you have got the hang of it, you can either take the plunge and start your own consultancy or join a large company as an 'internal' PRO. This can lead to a very well paid and powerful job dealing with top management and running a large, probably international, public relations department.

Banks

Banks are becoming more and more enlightened in their approach to women employees, having discovered that women are just as good at figures as men. There are a large number of women cashiers now and even one or two branch bank managers. If you enjoy arithmetic and dealing with money (remember it is much easier now, with calculators and computers at your fingertips) this could be a very good place to start. Most of the big banks have training schemes and at the moment there are nice perks too, such as help with your mortgage.

2
Escaping From Your Typewriter

There is a spirituality about the face . . . which the typewriter does not generate.

Sir Arthur Conan Doyle (1859-1930)

Assuming that you have found a company which you find congenial and in which you feel there is a chance for you to make your mark, don't be in too much of a hurry. Survey the scene and learn as much about the company's operations as you can.

What sort of man is at the top? Do his policies strike you as being on the right lines? What is his background? Who are the directors? What are their qualifications? And what do the employees think of them?

If it's a family business, is it being efficiently run or do you suspect that the bosses are only there because they are related to the founder?

Broadly speaking, a company or an organization run by men who have arrived at the top by their own unaided efforts is likely to be more dynamic than one which has passed from father to son. Even if no family links are involved, the track record of your firm's directors should give you an idea whether they are professional businessmen or whether they are there because they were at school with the 'right' people and have arrived on the board through the old boy network.

Having decided that the organization, and the business in which it is engaged, has a future and is being efficiently run, start to lay your plans.

The head of personnel for a big company once told me that when executives (male) were looking for someone to fill a job (as opposed to someone to fill a bed) it was as though their eyes wandered over a department without seeing the female members of the staff. They seemed to have a kind of cut-out mechanism which enabled them to perceive males only.

At the next desk might be a female graduate with a perfectly good brain, but somehow she didn't register. She was sitting at a typewriter, the office equivalent of the kitchen sink. In the home a female's role is cooking, in the office, typing.

This kind of superimposed 'camouflage' is something which females have got to break out of, if they want men to see them in a different light.

If you were a bright young man, you could feel fairly confident of getting spotted sooner or later and given the chance to show your potential.

You, in your female 'camouflage', cannot afford to be so complacent. You may have to draw yourself to your boss's attention as a possible candidate next time he is looking round for someone to take on a job with some prestige attached to it.

He may show mild surprise at such 'unfeminine' pushiness, but he might think you're worth the chance. If not this time, maybe next time around.

In the end he may feel you're so keen, it might be an idea to get you out of the office for a bit.

Getting around the company or out into the field will all help to round out your experience. When you get back, write a report – not too long-winded, you don't want to bore people – bringing out any points that you think should be mentioned. It may end up in your boss's wastepaper basket but it's all good practice.

If you're not getting anywhere with this plan you may find that you may have to move sideways for a start, rather than upwards.

Get to know as many people as you can and keep a sharp lookout for any vacancies that occur in divisions where you know there is a rapid turnover in the executive staff. That may be the department where you have the best chance of getting on. Persuade your boss that you would be happier in this other division. If necessary try to get the personnel department on your side. Plead incompatibility with your boss, or boredom with your job. Say that it's too undemanding.

If the man you are working for is not on a very high level, you may need to try and get *him* promoted to increase your own status. A man's efficiency increases in direct ratio to that of his secretary and it is up to you to make him seem brighter than he is. Make sure that his memos and letters are intelligible and to the point, even if you have to rewrite them yourself. You may have to prod him from time to time and generally keep him up to the mark. This will work to your advantage when you want to move on, as he will be quite relieved to get rid of you and sink back into his customary torpor.

After a while suggest that he needs a PA rather than a secretary, and try to get the personnel department to recommend you for a personal assistant's course.

This may not add up to much, but it will increase your status to that of PA, which is a step in the right direction. You are loosening the bonds which tie you to the typewriter.

Having become an 'assistant' you are only one jump away from your goal – an executive position. However junior you may be in the hierarchy, this is the essential breakthrough. No hurdle ahead of you will ever be quite as tough as this.

Because being a secretary is regarded as a dead-end job you have had to plot and plan to get away from it, but you will be living proof to others that it can be done.

It is unlikely that anyone will have helped you. You will have had to make every move yourself.

Now that you have reached base camp, as a PA, it is time to take another look at the serried ranks of male executives stretching out above you.

Start with your boss.

The proportion of really intelligent people in the population is pretty small. From the law of averages, therefore, you can safely assume that your boss is not there because he has brains, or even because he is the ideal person for the job, but for a number of other reasons. He is reasonably honest, reasonably reliable, but above all he was available, and he was a MAN.

You may say these qualifications don't add up to much and you would be right.

There might have been any number of other people including women, who could have done the job equally well.

Having satisfied yourself that your boss is almost certainly less intelligent than you are, don't waste time feeling resentful because this idiot is in a position of importance.

Knowledge is power and you have already discovered the truth about your superiors.

They're not as clever as they make out.

You will soon find your opinion confirmed when you study some of the decisions made by your masters. Never be tempted again to think that they know best. Come to your own conclusions. They are at least as likely to be right.

Depending on the size of your company, the number of grades you will have to pass through will vary. The group of men to whom your boss belongs is probably what is known as middle management, then senior management, followed by members of the board itself, the company directors who actually run the business.

In a well-run company there is constant movement and flexibility. As men retire they are replaced on the board. Promising young executives are being moved around from one subsidiary company to another or from one country to another around the world.

This continuous movement presages well for you, if in spite of your female 'camouflage' you can somehow manage to catch the eye of the management.

How to tackle these men who stand between you and the top jobs should be your next preoccupation.

The higher the level at which you can make an impression the better. Here you have an advantage. You may have suffered from female 'camouflage' as a secretary in the past, but once on the edge of the executive scene you will stand out like a beacon.

After the publicity given to the Equal Opportunities Bill most companies are more or less conscious of the lack of females in the hierarchy. It's a problem which they usually put aside on the principle of out of sight, out of mind, but there you are, a lone female in this vast concourse of males and it is impossible for the men who make the decisions not to notice you. If you get the impression that they're still ignoring you, make sure you *are* noticed.

Next time there is an occasion where junior members of the staff are admitted, such as a briefing meeting by the head of your department, ask a question or even go up and introduce yourself, after the meeting is over. This may look very pushy to the rest of your colleagues but what on earth have you got to lose? You're already an odd woman out, so your behaviour shouldn't be too surprising. After all there are no precedents for the actions of embryonic female executives at company meetings.

A seed will have been sown. Has this woman got executive potential? Shouldn't we at least give her a chance?

You have opened a door in their minds. Make sure you keep your foot inside it and don't let them forget that you exist.

3
How To Be an Executive

Pride goeth before destruction, and an haughty spirit before a fall.
Proverbs 16:18
Nobody Likes a Jumped-Up Secretary.
Anon.

Let us assume that at long last your plans have succeeded and you have been appointed a junior executive.

You may have been called in by your boss and given the good news. Your new status may be the result of joining a new company in answer to an advertisement. Whatever the route you have followed, your foot is on the bottom rung of the ladder. Your typewriter is a thing of the past.

The number of people delighted by your promotion will be strictly limited. So don't run around expecting to be congratulated and patted on the head.

'In the misfortunes *even* of our friends there is something far from unpleasing,' remarked that old cynic la Rochefoucauld, and there is some truth in this.

So if even your friends have mixed feelings, you may assume your enemies will be thoroughly annoyed at your success.

If you've played your cards right, you shouldn't have too many of the latter, but don't give people an excuse to say 'The whole thing's gone to her head.'

Above all, don't go rushing up to the first female executive you meet, expecting her to welcome you joyfully to the club as a new member.

She may not see it that way.

Interviews with a number of top women in business have revealed that the majority do not accept that there has been any discrimination against them, and are horrified at the idea of being identified in any way with a banding together of females, or any suggestion that they sympathize with what the media call 'bra-burning women's libbers'.

Reasons for these strong reactions are complex.

The women who say they've never encountered any discrimination and can't think what all the fuss is about, are usually possessed of the most enormous self-confidence, often the result of very strong early support and encouragement from parents, particularly fathers.

A man who only has a daughter will sometimes treat her as a son, giving her all the attention and devotion she needs to give her a head start in life.

She has probably never experienced the self-doubt that most of us feel from time to time, and sees herself on equal terms with *anyone*, and confidence we know is the key factor in any successful career.

So, all in all, if you feel like performing a victory dance over your new status, keep it to the privacy of your own home. In any case, nothing is in worse taste than gloating publicly over one's own success.

It may even cause your masters to wonder whether they have done the right thing in promoting you.

Keep a low profile until you have had time to settle in and assess your surroundings. 'Time spent on reconnaissance is never wasted' (old army saying).

First of all let's look at the basic necessities.

The Office

It is unlikely that you will get an office to yourself immediately, but it is important to start considering the layout at once – with an eye to the future.

You may have to begin in an open-plan office. These are going out of fashion, but there are still a number of them around. They have several disadvantages. In spite of plants and screens, they mean that privacy, both aural and visual, is at an end.

It is much easier for other people to see if you are in or out, and the whole impression is one of a ghetto with the lower orders supervised by Big Brother.

Status-wise they are, of course, the bottom.

The thing to aim for is an office of your own (preferably with your secretary outside where you can see her when your door is open).

A corner office may seem ideal at first, but *not necessarily*. Check which way it faces before you make it your goal.

An office with a south or south-west aspect can turn into an oven in summer, specially if it has large windows. North or north-east is best. Check to see if there are blinds, and that there is an alternative to strip lighting. If there isn't one you can import an Anglepoise.

As you proceed upwards you will get more and more choice of furniture and fittings, but don't make the mistake of getting too grand too fast. It only attracts unfavourable comment and can lay you open to the charge of wasting the company's money for your own aggrandisement.

Small and cosy is the thing to aim for.

So when the time comes, give in gracefully and let your rival have that big corner office which faces south-west. He can sit there getting overheated and flustered, while you remain cool in your northern fastness.

Proximity to the Boss

Opinions differ as to the desirability or otherwise of this. It largely depends on several factors: what sort of a boss have you got? How intimate do you *want* to be with him? If he is the neurotic type who tends to keep dashing in and out of your office, better put some distance between you. If he is the quiet type, though, you will probably learn more by moving in closer to the local seat of power and decision-making.

Your Secretary

You may have to start by sharing a secretary, or you may find you haven't got one at all. The latter is almost preferable because no secretary likes being shared. Her priorities are confused and relationships tend to suffer, not only between you and your colleague but between you and the secretary herself. As in courting, two's company, three's a crowd.

Absenteeism - Acceptable Excuses For

A man who says he is 'popping out for a haircut' can safely stay away from his office for a couple of hours without comment. Not so a female.

Although all your lunch hours may be taken up with business meals, you will still be expected to look well-groomed and 'feminine' at all times.

If you announce that you are off to get your coiffure attended to, you run the risk of snide remarks like 'The trouble with women is they spend all their time at the hairdresser's.'

You're up against the illogical reactions of the male sex (see p. 68). In their book, a man at the barber's, is carrying out a necessary function, even if he is actually having a two-hour cut and blow-dry at some trendy crimper's. A woman is not. (A friend of mine with difficult hair always kept a 'crisis wig' in her desk drawer for emergencies.)

So what excuses *are* acceptable?

The following:

Taking the car to be serviced. Anything to do with cars is acceptable, the car being revered by men as a sacred object which takes priority over practically everything else.

Dental appointment.

Burst water pipe.

Family funeral.

Gas leak.

Shopping (but only at Christmas).

Medical check-up. Only to be used if you've run out of the others. The men in your office will assume either that you are about to have a baby or some sinister 'female' operation.

The following are unacceptable:

Hair appointments.

Shopping (except at Christmas).

Family illness. If your husband, child or any other relation is ill, watch out. If you take time off you will be accused of 'not putting the company first', a piece of character assassination you will find hard to live down.

If you are duty-bound to stay by a sick-bed, it is much safer to pretend that *you* are the one who has gone down with something.

This will lead to fewer complications in the long run. (Remember that an absence of more than three days requires a doctor's certificate to back it up.)

After your alleged illness, *don't* come back bouncing all over the place or your colleagues may become suspicious and simply wonder if you have been skiving.

Make sure to make it clear that what you've been away with is nothing more than tummy trouble (refer to it as 'food-poisoning'), flu or some other run-of-the-mill complaint.

Though men are frequently off work with nervous headaches, hangovers, backaches, ulcers or just plain old-fashioned nervous breakdowns, it will simply be put down to 'pressure' or 'overwork'. In your case any of these ailments would be described as 'female neurosis' or 'emotional instability', so don't risk it.

I once tried out the ploy that I was going to an exercise class to see what effect this would have on my colleagues. The first reaction was one of unease. Were they to infer that I was stealing a march by keeping fitter than the rest of them?

If you are over thirty you may find yourself on the end of a put-down such as 'Is it wise? Don't forget the *anno Domini*, old girl.'

Expenses

As an executive, you will be entitled to an expense account. The size of it will vary, according to your seniority or the nature of your job.

Marketing directors and public relations executives usually have more entertaining to do than, say, personnel managers.

Top directors will probably have all their private telephone bills paid by the company, as a perk, and on the assumption that a large percentage of their calls will be connected with business.

Further down, you may find that just the quarterly rental will be paid for you. You will then claim for your business telephone calls as part of your general business expenses incurred outside the office.

These include business entertaining, petrol for your car on official trips and any other items, such as your newsagent's bill, if you are required to take the papers at home.

Entertaining is, of course, the main area where expense accounts are traditionally 'fiddled'.

In Fleet Street, the fiddling of expenses is reluctantly accepted by managements as part of a journalist's way of life from time immemorial. Most journalists would be prepared to admit that the more unscrupulous of their fellows actually live on their expenses and leave their salaries in the bank.

A columnist friend of mine always said it took him half an hour to write his weekly piece, but the real hard work was the four hours he spent dreaming up his expenses.

For years finance departments of companies large and small have been racking their brains to find a way of stopping people from exploiting the organization's resources in this time-honoured way. Unfortunately for them, short of putting a private detective on your trail (which would probably cost more than you are fiddling), their quest is still a hopeless one, as I shall explain.

The finance department may suspect that you are up to no good, but once you have learnt how to carry out your frauds, they will be unable to prove that their suspicions are well-founded.

The more bills you can include to back up your claims, the happier the finance department will be. But alas, some of these bills can still not be what they seem.

If, for instance, you wickedly decide to take your boy friend out to dinner at the company's expense, all you have to do is claim back the amount of the bill and put it down to 'entertaining Joe Bloggs', Joe Bloggs being of course a business associate with whom you might quite legitimately have been doing business.

A happy freemasonry exists between expense account fiddlers, and in the unheard-of event that Joe Bloggs gets a call to check that he actually did have dinner with you on the night in question, he will back you up, assuming that you would do the same for him.

In fact no company spy would dare to check on you like this, for the simple reason that you could probably sue him for giving outsiders the impression that you are a crook. In any case, he is perfectly aware that Joe Bloggs would back you up anyway.

Obviously you must be careful to ensure that Joe Bloggs was at least in the country at the time of the dinner. (Should you decide, possibly for financial reasons, to embark on such a shady enterprise as expense account fiddling, remember that – as in extra-marital affairs – it is always advisable to stick as close to the truth as possible.)

Many a careless fiddler has come unstuck by putting down a name without ensuring that at least the person concerned was actually around at the time.

A famous writer on a Sunday newspaper told me he once came badly unstuck by carelessly putting down the name of a man who had been dead for two months.

Should something like this happen to you, keep calm. Before your expense claim goes to the accountants, it is usually approved by the head of your department.

He is probably quite aware of what is going on and may be up to a bit of it himself.

To his comment 'I thought Joe Bloggs was in Australia,' you should reply 'Oh dear, it's that silly girl. She's typed the wrong name in' or 'It's all so long ago, I must have got the dates mixed.'

Some restaurants used to give their regular customers false bills for nonexistent meals, but I believe this practice has had to be discontinued due to the complications of VAT.

Taxis and pubs do not give bills at all, so they provide fertile ground for the dedicated fiddler. Taking a bus and charging for a cab, claiming cash for large rounds of drinks that never were – these are standard tricks of the trade.

Another favourite dodge involves a team of people who are sent away to another part of the country to do a job.

Some friends of mine who had to attend a lot of conferences used to pile into a car and drive to their destination and back. Afterwards each would claim for a first-class rail ticket.

The accountant who had to pass their expenses told me sadly in a rare moment of confidence that he knew all about this outrageous behaviour but was of course powerless to prove it.

With all this fiddling going on under their noses, it is no wonder that the company accountants who have to deal with expenses become bitter and twisted. In a large organization you may never get to meet the person who deals with your own expenses. His department may not even be in the same building. In a smaller company you may get to know him quite well, but don't be surprised if he sometimes regards you with a beady eye.

Even if every bill you put in is absolutely genuine, he may still appear resentful. The tragedy is that accountants engaged on this kind of work very rarely have expense accounts themselves.

After going through your bills and observing that you have been lunching at the Savoy on smoked salmon and grouse, washed down with claret and vintage port, he will probably be off to the staff restaurant for steak pie and chips.

Even if your lunch was actually very heavy going, with you selling a deal to some tedious but powerful gentleman, even if it resulted in a highly profitable new contract or thousands of pounds' worth of free publicity for your company, your accountant friend will still compare your life-style with his and feel cheated.

He wouldn't be human if he didn't.

Business Lunches

An awful lot of nonsense is talked about these, the consensus of opinion being that they are fattening, time-wasting, and an excuse for businessmen to get stoned out of their minds at the company's expense.

No doubt some people do, as we have seen, abuse their privileges in this way. In my experience business lunches can be very useful in oiling the wheels of commerce, and should be used simply as an alternative, and more pleasant way of talking business than at the inevitable meetings and sessions at the office. Above all, they are good for you and they keep you slim. Rare Scotch beef, top quality fillet steak, Dover soles, the very best and freshest fruit and vegetables, strawberries and asparagus out-of-season, the kind of fruit salad that doesn't come out of a tin – all these can be yours. (No filling up with sandwiches, beer, chips and cheap carbohydrates for you.)

How else can one indulge in such costly, nourishing, non-fattening, high-protein food at someone else's expense? And actually do the company some good at the same time by cementing relationships with business contacts?

Question: 'Which is the best restaurant?'

Answer: 'The one where they know you best.'

To arrive unknown in a restaurant is bad enough. To arrive as an unknown woman is a catastrophe. Head waiters being the male chauvinist pigs they are, you will almost certainly be given the worst table and service to match, unless you insure against it.

Become a regular customer and don't be mean with the tips. At first you may feel shy at the thought of taking a man out and paying for him. You may imagine that a man is going to be embarrassed by being paid for by you. There may have been some hesitation in the past on the part of men, but believe me they have now taken to the idea like ducks to water. The vast majority of men are tickled pink at being wined, dined and paid for by a female. And the system is now completely accepted in all restaurants where expense account entertaining is done. (It is important not to overdo the motherly bit. Tradition has it that Mary Wells, of New York advertising fame, once lost a bright young prospective employee by grabbing the bill from him with the words 'Let Momma pay!')

Some head waiters, needless to say, are not too happy about this turn of events, and will often show their disapproval by pointedly presenting your change to your male guest.

There is another diehard reactionary on the restaurant staff. He is the wine waiter, and he may also try to put you in your place by asking your guest to taste the wine on the assumption that no female can possibly have a palate.

While on the subject you should always hand the wine list to your guest. Ten to one he will hand it straight back and let you choose. After years of one-upmanship by wine experts and wine waiters, most men are thoroughly nervous of the whole subject and will be only too pleased to let someone else stick their necks out and take responsibility.

How to Return from Lunch (1)

If you are late returning to the office after a protracted lunch, don't rush back into the building all flushed and dishevelled, like some fugitive from a bacchanalian orgy. Take your time. A few more minutes here or there aren't going to make all that difference.

Enter the building calmly, wear tinted glasses if you feel you are looking a bit squiffy, make for the ladies' and check that your hair and make-up are as they should be.

Then walk coolly back into your office, preferably wearing an expression of deep thought, as though you are mulling over the weighty matters you have been discussing over lunch. (Proximity to your boss's office is a factor here. If you have chosen well, you should be able to slip in unnoticed by him.)

How to Return from Lunch (2)

Managements become suspicious when they realize that two or more of their executives have been lunching together.

They may feel fearful that a plot is being hatched, or that the bill is being fiddled, so never return to the office after lunch in company with colleagues.

In any case it is not always advisable to advertise the fact that you are on lunching terms with certain people.

Who your particular cronies or partners in crime are is *your* business. Therefore make some excuse, like urgent shopping, or a visit to the loo, so that you arrive separately in your respective offices.

Short Guide to Wine

In case you didn't know, there are three basic wines, red, white and rosé. Red wine is drunk with meat, game and poultry. In theory, white wine and rosé are drunk with fish.

But it is of no importance. Be prepared to flout convention. If you fancy red wine with your fish, go ahead and ignore the traditional rules. The general opinion is that French wines are the best, although the Italians and the Germans would probably disagree. So should you decide on something French, when given the wine list, if you feel like a red, go for the section marked Bordeaux and choose a cheap one, which is likely to be only three or four years old.

If you feel like a white wine, find the section headed Loire and pick one not more than four years old.

If there are no Loire wines on the list, choose one of the White Burgundies, but these will be considerably more expensive.

Beware White Bordeaux. It constitutes a positive minefield and can turn out to be extremely sweet.

If you do not like dry wines, choose a rosé. One of the best of these is Rosé d'Anjou. Rosé is usually demi-sec, which means half dry, but with a touch of sweetness in the background.

As far as Italian wines are concerned, if choosing a red look out for Chianti which everyone knows about, and for Barolo and Barbaresco, the two best reds from Piemonte. For a white wine you will not go far wrong with Soave from the Verona hills, or a Frascati from the Alban hills just outside Rome.

Germany produces a mass of fine wines, the best known of which is hock which gets its name from the Hockheim vineyards. Many of them are scented and flowery and if venturing into this field it might be wise to consult the wine waiter. Or there's always that old stand-by Liebfraumilch.

Portugal's best wine is port. And it doesn't have to be vintage.

Finally, remember that an extensive knowledge of wine can only be obtained through a lifetime of experience.

One should not ignore champagne. It certainly looks impressive, but on no account ask for a swizzle stick to remove the bubbles which have been imprisoned in the bottle at vast expense.

The champagne merchants say that it can be drunk before, during and after a meal. But there is a strong school of experts which says that it should be drunk at eleven in the morning and forgotten as soon as you sit down to luncheon.

A note on wine waiters: in expensive establishments they can sometimes be trusted to point out a bargain, because the management employs them full time. They will have passed examinations on wine.

In small restaurants and bistros it is safer to ignore their advice. Chances are they won't know what they're talking about. There are exceptions of course.

A lot of nonsense is talked about the *temperature* of wine. Traditionally, red wine would be served 'chambré', that is, at room temperature, whereas white and rosé should be slightly chilled. If you like your red wine cold, and some people do, why not? If you find that the white wine is not cold enough for you, ask for some ice to be put in it.

The wine waiter will pretend to be horrified at such female vandalism, but unless the wine is 'grand cru', and astronomically expensive, little harm will be done to it.

Do not bother too much about the specific year the wine was produced.

Finally, as an act that seldom fails to impress, when the waiter pours a drop into your glass for you to taste, just wave your hand to indicate that you are sure it's fine and not 'corked' and that he should fill your guest's glass without further ado.

He may insist on pouring the wine for your male guest to taste.

What your guest does, is naturally up to him.

You can then assess his level of sophistication by seeing if he's a 'taster' or a 'waver'. (Or a crafty glutton, who takes the chance to get one gulp's start on you.)

If you have become interested in wine, then buy a book on the subject, and endless hours of pleasure lie before you, together with a new language, often deliciously pretentious.

(I suppose the most famous 'pseudo' wine remark is 'I detect a slight malevolence in the *au revoir*,' from Stephen Potter's well-known spoof on the subject – 'Winemanship'.)

Tipping in Restaurants

Most restaurants now include the tip in the price of the meal. If the tip hasn't been added on, you will see the words 'service not included' as a gentle hint.

A lot of people seem to panic when deciding how much to tip. You can easily work it out, using 10 per cent as your basic guide.

All you have to do is move the decimal point one digit to the left.

If the bill comes to less than £10 (unlikely these days) say £8.50, move the point to the left. This will give you 0.85p or 85p which is 10 per cent. You can then make up the amount to the nearest round figure, or more if you are feeling generous.

Say the bill is £24.40, again move the point to the left. This gives you £2.44, which again is 10 per cent. If the bill is £125.60, you will get £12.56 and so on.

If you have such a blind spot about figures that the thought of moving a decimal point in any direction whatever gives you the vapours, invest in a small pocket calculator, and let it do the sum for you.

They are so simple to use that even the most non-numerate person can feel secure in the knowledge that their calculations are correct, once they have learnt which buttons to press.

Foreign Travel

As an executive, even a fairly junior one, you will almost certainly find yourself being sent abroad for some reason or other.

The commonest activity involving travel is the attending of conferences.

'When in doubt, hold a conference', seems to be the motto of top executives all over the world these days, and of course conference-holding is enthusiastically encouraged by airlines, travel agents, hotels and conference centres and all the other organizations and groups of people who stand to make a profit out of it.

You will either be travelling to a foreign city to help organize a conference which your company is sponsoring, or you will have been delegated to attend somebody else's conference on your company's behalf. This usually means that nobody among the top brass is specially keen to attend this particular shindig, but they feel that someone ought to go, so it might as well be you.

Or you may be going to attend a policy meeting which is being held by one of your company's overseas subsidiaries, and you are being sent to attend the meeting and report back on some aspect of its activities to your superiors.

The days when air travel abroad on business was a prestige activity are over. Every Tom, Dick and Harry now flies overseas as a matter of course, and passengers on the airlines of the world now look more like a crowd of commuters on the London Underground, than the cream of the international business community on the move. Gazing round the departure lounge you might be forgiven for imagining that you are on a platform on the Bakerloo Line on a wet weekday morning.

It isn't even very comfortable, you will probably have to hump your own luggage, or push it on a trolley, porters being practically nonexistent. So do travel light.

The worst part of air travel to my mind, is the hanging around in 'lounges', with no idea what time your plane will *actually* leave the ground. For non-smokers it is particularly unpleasant, as the table you are 'lounging' at is almost invariably adorned with an ashtray full of old cigarette stubs, a nauseating sight, especially first thing in the morning.

The second nastiest thing about flying, unless you are one of the elite who goes first class (see page 77), is the lack of leg-room in a modern jet.

Speaking as a five foot two, seven stone midget, I find it almost impossible to imagine the sufferings of those over six foot, over twelve stone people who have to squeeze themselves into the space provided by airlines for the accommodation of the human frame in transit.

Babies (crying) or children (scrambling over one's lap) are also in-flight hazards.

The food, of course, rather like that provided by motorway cafés, has become a bit of a national joke, but I usually find that there is at least one item among the ingeniously designed display of provender which is edible. The rest one may take back to amuse one's relations and some of the plastic containers make very good homes for geranium cuttings.

The hotel, when you get to it, will almost certainly be one of the anonymous, international links in a vast American chain.

The whole impression is one of being packaged and processed like a frozen chicken. Except that you will soon be de-frosted and boiled alive by the central heating.

The windows will be almost impossible to open. Having opened one, you will be prevented from shutting it by a force nine gale. Should you have time, between your arrival and your first appointment, to summon the staff to carry out these man-oeuvres on your behalf, don't be surprised if they regard you as a dangerous lunatic. They may try to humour you by turning down the heating, but ask them to tackle the windows at your peril.

Your room will have been designed for occupation by a quick succession of tall businessmen. You will very likely have to stand on tip-toe to see your face in the bathroom mirror, and don't rely on finding a full-length one – or enough coat hangers.

On the plus side you will have a private bath, a telephone, radio and TV channels galore.

In Europe, you may be diverted to discover some old favourite TV serial dubbed into the local language.

Best of all, you will have room service.

The Americans are very good at room service and the staff at these hotels actually seem to enjoy being rung up at all hours of the day and night and asked to supply you with food and drink. In most hotels there is also a drinks cupboard so that you can help yourself.

If you are a lone female staying at any hotel, you will have to face the problem of whether to go down alone to dinner. Head waiters are the same the world over, and as an unaccompanied female, and a foreigner to boot, you will be plonked down in the middle of the room and left there. You may well find that you are the only woman in sight. The others, if any, will have male escorts or be in a large party.

Unless you are a complete masochist, therefore, you may well be daunted by this bleak prospect.

This is where room service comes into its own. Make yourself comfortable in your bedroom, and order a slap-up dinner to be brought to you. Ordering half a bottle of champagne to be sent up to you *before* dinner, will help convince the staff that you mean business.

If, due to some administrative mix-up, you are forced to stay in a hotel without room service, take a book with you to the restaurant and read it assiduously throughout your meal. A paperback copy of *War and Peace*, or any other classic you've always been meaning to find time for, will do nicely.

Tipping in Hotels

Tips are now almost universally included in the bill in the international hotels you are likely to be patronizing, but in the unlikely event that you require any extra-mural services such as tickets for the opera or an expert guide to take you round the sights, it is advisable to give a large tip to the hall porter, or 'bell captain', as the Americans picturesquely call him.

Sightseeing?

It is most unlikely that during your trip abroad you *will* have any time to admire the scenery or visit the tourist attractions

The cliché that executives on business trips abroad see nothing but airport lounges, conference rooms and hotel bedrooms wherever they go is all too true.

So travel abroad is no picnic. Why bother? Because travelling abroad is an essential ingredient in your business career. Not to have visited the company's plant in Frankfurt or the American subsidiary will put you at a disadvantage status-wise. You will have to go through the whole distasteful process sooner or later.

It is in fact essential for practical purposes to meet the staff of the overseas companies. You may need their support in the future, and the more of the top brass you get to know world-wide the better. There is nothing like personal contact to win people on to your side. At the company's international conferences, you should eventually be able to greet most of the delegates by their christian names, having already met them on their own home ground, a big advantage. Among those overseas executives are almost certainly the future directors of the company. The young man at present doing his stint abroad may be already earmarked as a possible chief executive.

Asking for a Rise

Even strong men blench at the thought of walking into their boss's office and asking for more money.

Why this should be so, I don't know. After all, the worst the boss can do is say no.

I think it must have something to do with masculine pride.

A man is afraid that he will lose face with the boss by having to demean himself in this way.

It's bad enough having to go cap in hand to ask for a rise.

It's even more humiliating to be refused.

This fear is catching, and women, already suffering from lack of confidence, and tending to undervalue themselves anyway, are even more cowardly when it comes to hinting that an increase in salary would be appropriate.

A lot depends on the boss of course, and on your relationship with him.

If it's fairly informal, you can try the 'Indirect Request'.

This involves making your point in a throwaway line, tagged on to the end of a casual conversation.

Thus, 'Good Morning, Mr Bloggs. Isn't the weather awful? I've just been finishing my Christmas shopping. Everything seems to cost the earth. Any chance of a bit more cash in the New Year?'

By observing his reactions closely, you can gauge what your chances are, and whether it's worth pressing the point further.

If he says, 'Well, I can't promise anything, but you never know' or something like that, the matter may be worth pursuing at a later date.

If he just looks embarrassed, you can assume the answer is likely to be no.

On the other hand, he is now aware that you are expecting a rise, and he may start to wonder if he ought to do anything about it.

Because women are traditionally paid less than men, their bosses very rarely put the salaries of female executives at the top of their list of priorities, so you've given him a jog in the right direction.

If he says, 'Not a hope, my dear, we've all got to tighten our belts you know', or 'You'll be lucky!' you can forget about the matter for at least another six months.

If your relationship with your boss is less relaxed, your timing and technique will have to be immaculate.

Again, the indirect approach is recommended. It is preferable to bring up the subject at the end of a meeting with your boss, at which you have been discussing other matters, rather than attack it head on. As you get up to leave his office, say, 'By the way, I hope you don't mind my mentioning the sordid subject of finance, but I have been incurring rather a lot of expense lately. (Mention moving house, or settling your aged mother in an expensive nursing home. Problems with elderly parents are always a good bet, giving the right impression of you as a Dutiful Daughter.) I was wondering if there was any chance of a bit more money in the future?'

This will strike the correct note, giving him the chance to take up the fatherly attitude so popular among male executives when dealing with females in their charge. He will almost certainly launch into a little lecture about how bad times are and how difficult it is to give anybody a rise, but he will end by saying that of course he will bear you in mind and do what he can.

Thank him, looking suitably grateful and make a respectful exit.

By this time, your boss will be feeling not only fatherly but magnanimous. He may decide to show you how powerful he is by getting you that rise.

He will then call you in and say, 'Well my dear I've got some good news for you. *I've managed to get* you a bit more money,' inferring that only by using his considerable influence on your behalf has he been able to squeeze the extra cash out of his tight-fisted superiors. You are a lucky girl indeed, he will imply, to have such a friend at Court.

Should your boss be of an exceptionally nervous disposition, you will have to employ a different strategy altogether.

A really nervous boss can rapidly become hysterical at the mere mention of money, so timing is crucial if you are to avoid pushing him into a state of counter-productive panic.

Even the most neurotic men have some panacea which goes at least some way to allaying their fears. By observing your boss's moods, you will soon discover when he is at his most relaxed.

Such men often calm down when they are away from the office, so you may find him in a receptive state when you are both returning from some foreign trip.

Others become quite human when their own boss is away.

Others again, tend to mellow with lunch and are at their most approachable while sipping a post-prandial coffee. A large whisky-and-soda at the end of the day will sometimes work wonders.

Having chosen your moment, adopt a soothing tone and ask

him How, in *general terms*, does he see the company's financial future?

From the company's finances, it is only a step to the finances of your own department.

Having found a sympathetic ear, your boss will soon start describing his own problems with balancing his budget.

This is the *moment critique*.

Still keeping the atmosphere low-key, you should now observe philosophically, 'From what you are saying, I assume there isn't much chance of a rise for any of *us* this year.'

His reaction to this remark will tell you all you need to know.

The government pay guidelines have of course proved a godsend to beleaguered bosses trying to keep their rapacious staffs at bay.

Not many people actually understand the ramifications of these guidelines, and many an innocent girl has been fobbed off with the words, 'We'd simply *love* to give you a pay rise, but unfortunately as you know we are bound by the Government's Pay Policy.'

A lot of bosses don't understand these rules themselves, and the temptation to use the Government as an excuse for not paying people more must be very great.

The fact is that most companies can, and do, find ways of rewarding their top executives, *if they really want to*, pay guidelines or not.

If you suspect that you are being unfairly denied a pay rise, but keep coming up against a brick wall, there is help at hand.

Most executives have mixed feelings about whether trade unions are a 'good thing' or not. Certainly they are not noted for their efforts on behalf of their female members, but if you do happen to belong to one of the 'white collar' unions, or know someone who does, don't be too proud to ask their advice. The branch negotiators of these trade unions are experts in these pay policies. They know every detail of the law and they are by definition *on your side*. Explain the circumstances and you will soon have all the facts about your entitlement to promotion at your fingertips.

The next step is to ask your trade union friend to drop you

a line, setting out the facts, and explaining that there is no reason, *as far as the Government's policies are concerned,* why you should not receive your increase.

Now comes the tricky bit.

Managements, as we know, are uneasy about promoting women to higher jobs. They are even more nervous about trade unions. The combination of a woman asking for more money, backed by a trade union which says the law is on her side, may, unless carefully presented, result in heart attacks or worse among your superiors.

It is up to you to defuse the situation.

Approach your boss tactfully, and explain that you know he is trying to get you some more money, but that he is worried about the Government's policy, so you have decided that it might be helpful to get an independent opinion.

Here is a letter you say, which you *hope* may go some way towards solving the problem.

Leave the letter with him, and withdraw discreetly.

He knows as well as you do that union negotiators know their stuff.

Your pay increase should not be long delayed.

If you do not already belong to it, the union concerned may expect you to do the decent thing and become a member of it.

4
Friends and How
To Make Them

Acquaintance I would have, but when't depends not on the
number, but the choice of friends.

Abraham Cowley (1618-67)

Anybody attempting to climb the company tree needs all the
friends they can get. As a female, you are going to need them
even more. Apart from the obvious people in power with whom
you have to try and make your mark, there are a number of
other key categories among the staff whose goodwill and co-
operation can go a long way towards smoothing your way to the
top. Some of them may not at first sight appear 'important' but
their power to hamper operations is regularly underestimated
by 90 per cent of the executives in your company. Waste no
time – get them on your side.

Secretaries

The chances are that you yourself started off as a secretary and
this gives you the advantage of understanding how these essential members of the organization feel and work. Most men tend
to treat their secretaries with a degree of indifference which is
quite staggering. The commonest cause of complaint among
secretaries is that they don't feel involved and that their bosses
refuse to allow them any responsibility. I have come across
secretaries whose bosses do not even let them answer the telephone. No wonder these women become bored and resentful,
have their typewriter covers on and are out of the building by
5.31 sharp every day of the week.

The men for whom these women work often express mild
surprise at their lack of interest in the job, but put it down to

the changing times we live in, talking nostalgically of the good old days when women had a 'sense of duty' and were prepared to work all hours of the night for the sake of the company. The words Dedication and Loyalty are bandied about and there is much shaking of heads among older executives over the disrespectful way in which these flighty females carry out their duties. Treated as fellow human beings, secretaries, especially other people's, can be very useful allies.

They read their bosses' post and type their letters and they often know, through the secretarial underground, a lot more about what is going on in the department than their bosses do. They don't have any illusions about their bosses either and they can be quite devastatingly frank. One particular man insisted on inspecting every form and piece of paper however trivial before it left the department.

'Why does he want to see all these things?' I asked his secretary.

'It makes him feel important,' she said crisply.

A secretary knows when is the best time for you to approach her boss. She knows his moods and foibles, whether he is a better bet before or after lunch. This can vary quite widely among your colleagues. Some are a push-over at 8.30 in the morning. Others are like bears with sore heads until they have had their midday meal, or their first drink of the day. All this information is useful if you are planning to ask a favour, and your friend the secretary will be glad to supply it.

You should also keep an eye on your secretary as potential executive material. Many a bright girl has been discovered camouflaged behind her typewriter.

Your own secretary is of course of paramount importance. The days when secretaries refused to work for women are I hope on the way out. Mainly, I think, because the old-fashioned 'battle-axe' type of lady executive, like the old-fashioned 'dedicated' secretary, is disappearing from the scene.

These old battle-axes (like the old secretaries) were probably of sterling worth, hard-working, loyal and usually exploited. They were probably worth their weight in gold to the company, although they were doubtless treated as a joke by their male colleagues. Some men still tend to cringe in mock terror when they hear that they are going to have to deal with some as yet unseen 'high-powered' female executive.

None of these old battle-axe ladies ever reached the top and they were doubtless passed over many times in favour of less talented men. I bet these ladies gave their secretaries hell, because they were perfectionists. They had to be to prove they were as good as the men. Most of them were unmarried. Or rather they were married to the company they served, and got put out to grass, kindly one hopes, when the time came. One still comes across these rare pioneers in the cause of female equality, though they probably didn't see it in that way. They are often indefatigable travellers and gardeners and fiercely independent. But they must indeed have been tough to work for.

If you can make your secretary your friend, you will find that you will have a very successful working partnership. Don't ever make the mistake of your male colleagues and treat her like a shorthand-typing machine. Take her into your confidence as much as possible. Tell her what is going on, and what the plans and policies are relating to the work in which you are both involved. Don't be too dogmatic about her time-keeping. If you have got yourself the right person, she will not grudge doing a bit extra when it's really needed. Give her a chance to use her brain. Ask her advice. It will be well worth having and you will find she is one of your greatest allies, a staunch supporter in your bid for the top.

If she is ambitious, don't try to hold her back. Encourage her in her ambition. She could become your assistant and even perhaps an executive in her own right. You will then have an even more powerful friend on your side.

The idea of losing this treasure may at first seem unwelcome, but there are plenty of bright girls around and with the help and advice of the secretary who is moving on you can soon train the new one up to the standard you require, if you have chosen wisely.

Not every secretary however *wants* to move up in the world. She is often quite happy to carry on in her job so long as it gives her satisfaction and she doesn't feel bored. It's up to you to see that she isn't. That's what good boss/secretarial relations are all about.

Fellow (for Want of a Better Word) Female Executives

In a large company, the few, if any, female executives are likely to be thinly spread around in various areas of the organization, and may not come across each other very often.

When they do meet, either at some group function or in the ladies' loo, they tend to view each other rather warily. I don't know why this should be. There is a tradition that woman don't naturally flock together. Maybe because in a male-dominated society women are brought up to be suspicious of each other. Something to do perhaps with the well-proved policy of 'divide and rule', also known as the 'my man comes first' syndrome. Whatever the reason, men certainly like to foster the idea that women can't get on together in business. It's known as the Queen Bee theory which suggests that any woman will automatically destroy a rival as soon as she appears. (This is quite contrary to male behaviour. A small number of males isolated in a predominantly female group automatically band together 'for protection' as they put it in their jokey way.)

It's well worth making the effort to get to know your female colleagues if you are lucky enough to have any. After all, you've got a lot in common and another woman on your level can be a sympathetic confidante.

It may be that there is a lone lady lawyer in the legal department or a remote female director on the board of one of the subsidiary companies. There is probably a woman or two in the PR department, though the head of the department will ninety-nine times out of a hundred be a man. There will almost certainly be a lady personnel officer somewhere in the organization. Personnel, at least on the middle levels, has always been thought of as a woman's job. There seems to be something in the theory that women are often encouraged to do the jobs that don't particularly interest men, so presumably men just never wanted to get into that particular scene.

Now that employee communications is the name of the game, maybe some of these middle-ranking personnel women will rise nearer the top.

All these women can be useful to you and you, in your specific job, may be useful to them. They may well become your personal friends.

One thing you have to face up to. However hard you try, however successful you may be in getting yourself accepted as part of the team, you can never really become 'one of the boys'. Men never quite seem able to realize that a woman, however much they may like and get on with her, is actually a member of the same species, a fellow human being. When the crunch comes, a man will always retreat to his cosy all-male group. Like a lot of male behaviour, it remains a mystery, though various theories have been put forward.

Sad though it is, it must be accepted as one of the facts of life, at least in our particular Anglo-Saxon society. However, more and more women are discovering that other women can be very good company, and this can only bode well for the future.

Company Wives

Most male executives have an ambivalent attitude to the wives of their superiors. On the one hand they suspect these ladies of exerting too much (of the wrong sort of) influence over their husbands. On the other, they tend to treat them in an exaggeratedly obsequious fashion at official functions, on the theory that it might just help their plans for self-advancement.

At worst these wives are looked upon as an irritating nuisance, a sort of cross to bear. Some chairmen do sometimes quote their wives' opinions at meetings and this is usually greeted with deep sighs and knowing looks by those present.

The top man's wife in fact may be the main ingredient in her husband's success. Very few successful men have made it without the support and sometimes the active push of their wives.

Bearing this in mind, the chances are that a director's wife is an interesting person in her own right. It is certainly worth finding out. Most wives of members of top management are delighted to meet and make friends with women executives employed by their husband's company. After years of having to make conversation with men who aren't really interested in her for herself, or their wives who are probably too much in awe of her to behave naturally, it is a refreshing change for her to meet a woman executive who is high enough up in the company to be able to talk the language, and who can chat to her woman-to-woman on her own level. Most top wives are keenly interested in their husband's company, but only hear his side of things. They are dying to get the low-down, and you as an independent agent can give her another perspective on company affairs, though it is obviously very important not to abuse your position as the boss's wife's confidante. Discretion is the watchword. But it is possible to build up the relationship to your mutual benefit. You can keep her in touch with grass roots feelings in the company, which if she likes she can pass on to her husband. Through her you can keep in touch with her husband's opinions and attitudes, whether he enjoyed his holiday – whether he is having problems with his relations, or how he feels about the latest government decisions. Knowing other dimensions of the men who run the business and the women behind them is part of your job. The better you know them and what makes them tick, the more effectively you will be able to carry out your own role within the company.

Homosexuals

According to statistics, at least 3 per cent of the male population is exclusively homosexual.

This means that up to three or more of every hundred men in your organization may be of this persuasion.

It is a common misconception that all homosexuals are

clustered together in such 'creative' fields as showbiz and the arts.

It is probably true that there is a higher percentage of the more obvious ones in these areas where less prejudice exists, but they are also to be found, though heavily disguised, throughout business and industry, some of them at the highest levels.

Because of the prejudice which still exists against them in these more conservative areas of the community, they are careful not to advertise their presence, keeping their personal lives to themselves and conforming outwardly as much as possible in appearance and behaviour with their heterosexual colleagues.

They will hint that they have a girl friend, and be careful either to come alone or to bring a woman friend (or 'cover-girl' as they are known) to company functions where wives are included in the invitation.

They may adopt such 'masculine' habits as pipe-smoking and you may even find one posing as 'Superpocket' and giving you the 'eye treatment' (see next chapter).

It is not surprising that under all this camouflage, these 'closet queens', as they are sometimes called, are virtually undetectable, except to the expert eye.

It will be well worth your while to track down these treasures, for that is what they are.

Most homosexual men like and get on very well with women, with whom, after all, they have a lot in common.

Unlike most businessmen, they are very good company. Once they realize that you have guessed the truth about them and are not the slightest bit perturbed by it, they will become your confidants, letting down their hair in the privacy of your office and keeping you amused and entertained with endless anecdotes about your more pompous colleagues.

They will provide a welcome bit of light relief after the heavy-going proceedings which make up most of your office routine.

Once they have learned to trust you, knowing that their secret is safe in your hands, they will become charming allies and friends for many years to come.

45

'Gay' Clues

Nowadays long hair and trendy clothes make 'gay' spotting much more difficult than before.

Through the influence of the pop world, however 'normal' a man may actually be, he may sometimes consider it to be the 'in' thing to appear 'camp'.

In a society where even bricklayers and juggernaut drivers sport necklaces, earrings and high-heeled clogs, life does sometimes get confusing.

However there are clues, though I must stress that no single one, or even all, of these characteristics can be described as conclusive evidence. They are only a guide, signs which may repay further investigation.

Bachelor status.

Preoccupation with appearance and grooming.

Trendy clothes and hair-styles, especially in the middle-aged.

Discreet jewellery, such as gold bracelets or ornate cufflinks.

Appreciation of ballet, opera and the theatre.

Fondness for name-dropping.

Reticence about personal life.

Use of expressions like 'my dear'.

Receptionists

These are almost invariably female. They can range from elderly 'dragons' whom men dare not sack because they are so efficient, to 'dolly-birds' who have been chosen to 'decorate' the foyer and make what the management think is a good impression on the male executives who come to visit the company

Whatever type they may be, their co-operation is vital, so cultivate them assiduously. If you don't, you run the risk that urgent parcels and messages will sit indefinitely on their desks or important visitors may be kept hanging about while you fume and fret upstairs, wondering what is holding up the action. Getting your secretary to ring down every five minutes to find out if the urgent parcel or the important visitor are sitting downstairs doesn't work, because receptionists' telephones are always engaged, often, one must admit, with private conversations. But don't get too stern with them. You need them more than they need you, so always say good morning, and have a chat when you've got time.

Commissionaires

There are commissionaires and commissionaires. The really grand ones, who belong to the Corps, are used to opening doors for the Highest in the Land, and expect to be treated accordingly. They are elderly and conservative, though not above having a quick 'nip' round the corner or a visit to the betting shop. A bottle of whisky at Christmas will usually ensure that a taxi will be summoned at your bidding and a large umbrella unfurled next time you step out into a downpour.

Even if your company can only run to a common or garden 'security man', the treatment should be the same.

Chauffeurs

Chauffeurs, it is commonly agreed, know more about what is going on than anybody else outside the board of directors. How? Simple. They drive their bosses around to all sorts of meetings in all sorts of different locations and they hear all the conversations which go on in the backs of their cars.

It's amazing how indiscreet top executives can be in front of (or rather behind) their drivers. Is a top secret merger brewing? Is some eminent politician about to join the board? Is such and such a famous company on the verge of collapse? The chauffeurs are the first people to get wind of it. Though they don't always understand the implications of their knowledge, there's no doubt that they've got it. The real test of how secret a top secret is, is do the chauffeurs know? If they don't then it really is a secret.

I am not suggesting that you should waste your time trying to piece together like a jigsaw the various bits of information collected from the chauffeurs in your organization. Life is too short and anyway that sort of knowledge isn't really worth having unless you're fiddling on the Stock Exchange, which I don't recommend. It's far too easy to come unstuck and even chauffeurs can get the wrong end of the stick.

The main reason why chauffeurs are your friends is that they can squeeze you into the company car park, even clean your car if they're in the mood, and they always know where their bosses are, and where and when they are going. So if you want to get on with something in the certain knowledge that the chairman or the managing director is out of the way, you'll know who to ask.

Chauffeurs, for some reason, seem to be particularly flirtatious, something to do with the effect of constant movement on the human frame I believe. So don't get trapped in the garage with a chauffeur unless you really fancy him.

The Post Room

People who work for the post room spend their time in an endless spiral, walking round and round the building delivering and collecting post and parcels. They nearly always seem to be male, though they never need to carry anything heavier than a large envelope. They usually suffer with their feet and are called Jo or Len. Get on christian name terms as soon as you can and you will find them among the most helpful and friendly of mortals. There is always one man in charge of the post room and he is of vital importance when you want to get something urgent into the last post. A crate of beer at Christmas and a sympathetic ear at all times are appreciated by the post room staff.

Messengers

Most large companies have a 'stable' of messengers who run errands, usually in vans, between the various company locations. They're also expected to get the evening papers for those executives who are entitled to them and generally make themselves useful delivering urgent messages and communications *as requested*. I use the phrase advisedly, because it depends who is doing the requesting. If you treat the messengers as your friends and don't try to order them about, they will oblige you in all sorts of ways and will make life that much easier when you are desperately trying to get some document up to the City or down to the lawyers at top speed and there isn't a taxi or despatch rider to be had. They may even give you a lift in their van to an urgent appointment.

The Man in Charge of the Building

The man in charge of the building usually has a title of some sort like Administration Manager, or Manager of Plant and Services, or something of the kind. What it boils down to is that he is the man who decides what furniture (if any) you have in your office. His word is law (unless you are bent on beating the system) and it pays to keep on the right side of him at all times. Failing to do so can result in the most miserable state of affairs such as being without a telephone, a decent desk, chairs, or even blinds on the windows or carpet on the floor. This may sound ridiculous but there is no end to the delays and excuses – the chair manufacturers are on strike, the delivery men are working to rule, the carpet company has gone bankrupt, the telephone engineers can't come until Wednesday – which can be trotted out by the man in charge of the building, should you have slighted him or failed to win his favour.

These unfortunate men have perhaps the worst job in the company. They are besieged by complaints and bedevilled with problems.

Everything that goes wrong, from the leak in the ladies' loo to the simultaneous failure of all the lifts in the building and the collapse of the chairman's air conditioning, is blamed on to them. It is a wonder that they can raise a smile at all. Yet amazing though it may seem they can be quite kind and helpful if treated with consideration and sympathy. If you can make him your friend, the MCB will make sure that your photocopier is always working, your chairs are soft, your secretary's type-writer is never out of order and your office is a haven of rest and comfort. It's up to you. And don't forget to say thank you. It will probably come as such a shock, he will be your friend for life.

The Cleaners

It is unlikely that you will ever come face to face with the cleaners. They are a nocturnal species, either creeping in to clean your office late at night or early in the morning before you come to work. The fact that you never see them doesn't mean that you shouldn't get them on your side. It must be very depressing to spend your life cleaning up after people you never see. Try not to leave your office looking like a rubbish heap with the wastepaper basket overflowing, dirty ashtrays and papers all over the floor. If you do, they will just give up and leave the whole mess much as it was and who is to blame them? If it is reasonably tidy, they might even polish your desk. It has been known.

Communications

Fast communications are the life-blood of any successful busi-ness. Telephone, switchboard and telex staff are therefore key figures in the efficient running of your operations whatever they may be. Make sure that the switchboard have your correct extension and your secretary's. Especially in a large company where people are frequently moving offices, it is no good relying on the admin. manager to ensure that everyone is correctly listed at all times. He's got quite enough to worry about without that sort of attention to detail.

Don't treat telephone girls like faceless slaves, or ring them to get overseas numbers for you when they are at their busiest (usually around late morning) or complain when they cut you off by mistake. If you do, it probably *won't be* by mistake next time you are on an important call.

Telex operators are also extremely important to you and your attitude towards them will decide whether they come up four floors with an urgent telex or whether it sits there for another half hour before you get it. If the telex operator offers to work overtime for you, make sure she has got transport home. Don't just take it for granted that she will get there somehow.

The man from the GPO is the most powerful figure of all in these vital communications. Terrible taboos exist which dictate that no other than he may lay a finger on your telephone or its cable.

The visits of this god-like personage are awaited with impatience.

Like primitive tribes scanning the skies for rain, frustrated executives peer down the corridors for his appearance. It may take weeks but one day he will arrive, carrying his magic case of equipment which means that your long-awaited extension is about to become operational or your defunct dialling system is about to start working. Knowledge of the enormous power he wields gives the Man from the GPO a wonderfully relaxed manner. He knows nothing can happen till he arrives so he proceeds at a leisurely pace. All will be attended to in due course. In the meantime what he really enjoys is a good gossip. If you can keep him amused while he makes the vital connection to the maze of wires spread out on your carpet, he may come back a bit earlier next time when you are *in extremis*. It's certainly worth a try.

Tea Ladies

Just as messengers and post room workers nearly always seem to be male, so the people who push trolleys with tea and coffee round the building are almost invariably female.

Should you have got to the stage in your career when you are making your own coffee in the office, or getting your secretary to do it if she is agreeable, the trolley ladies will do the washing-up for you if properly approached. If you have become even grander and actually have a drinks cupboard, there is the problem of dirty glasses.

Again the trolley ladies will help out if the amount of crockery and glasses doesn't get too excessive. This saves your secretary from having to smuggle the whole lot out to the loo, with the always present hazard of losing a whole tray full of glasses and china if someone in a hurry comes rushing in the other direction through the ladies' room door.

The problem is a human one. The trolley ladies probably get more recognition from the office staff than other workers. Because they bring the longed-for refreshment in the morning or mid-afternoon, they are usually greeted with pleasure and are chatted up by the queue which quickly forms around them.

Nevertheless, they are almost certainly not on familiar terms with any executives, who, like you yourself, have made other arrangements more in keeping with your elevated position above the herd.

Go out of the way to have a word with the trolley lady on your floor and if necessary listen to her problems. She has almost certainly got them, as most of the women who do this work seem, like the night cleaners, to be married with children, or have to go out to work for some reason to earn extra money.

Extra cash is probably the best present, but you will have to feel your way in this one. A sympathetic ear may well be all that's expected of you, and suitable thanks from time to time

Your Boss

The friendship of your boss, whoever he (and in rare cases she) may be, is of course essential if you are going to lead a reasonably smooth existence in the office. Adopt a soothing manner and try to cause him as little aggravation as possible. If he's got an obsession about staff getting in on time, try to humour him in this respect. Don't rush in and out of his office with trivial problems when he's in the middle of planning his departmental budget for the next five years. Don't keep him chatting late in the evening when you know his wife likes to have him home for dinner by 7.30.

Don't groan when he comes in to see you with a pile of paperwork. Try and look cheerful and accept whatever he is going to unload on to you with a good grace. Don't drop hints about promotion or pay increases when you know he's already been badgered by his secretary about the way her train fares are going through the roof. As we have seen, there is a time and place to mention such things and you should choose your moment carefully. You may have to wait until you are both returning from a successful business lunch. Or until the office party when he's had a few drinks. Timing is everything, and you don't want to give the poor man ulcers on top of all the problems he's already got on his mind. It is to your advantage to keep him as happy and relaxed as possible. Nothing is more distracting than a neurotic boss.

As we have already established, your boss is almost certainly there because he is male and because he happened to be in the right place at the right time. By the nature of things, you are likely to be at least as bright as he is, so understanding and 'managing' him shouldn't be too difficult. If you've an intelligent boss, be grateful and make sure he is your friend.

5
Enemies and How
To Outwit Them

> We are bay'd about with many enemies;
> and some that smile, have in their hearts,
> I fear, millions of mischiefs.
> *Shukespeare,* Julius Caesar
> The height of cleverness is to be able to conceal it.
> *Duc de la Rochefoucauld (1613–80)*

If you've played your cards right and followed all the rules, you should in theory end up with no enemies at all, but there are always a few hard nuts to crack, some so uncrackable that in the long run you may have to 'work around' them before you can proceed onwards and upwards.

Your main stumbling block will almost certainly be the group described as middle-aged middle management. These tradition- ally constitute the most conservative and inflexible section of any organization.

Broadly speaking those men who have reached the top or who feel confident that it is only a matter of time before they do, tend to be relaxed, broadminded and generally out-going. They are receptive to new ideas such as the promotion of females to the higher grades, and it is most unlikely that they will go out of their way to impede your progress. Because they are self-confident, they are not so likely to regard you as a threat to their masculinity or their power.

The middle-aged middle management on the other hand tend to be set in their ways. The ones you will probably have trouble with are the ones who suspect that it is unlikely that they will get much further in the organization. The appearance of bright young male executives is bad enough. It tends to increase their insecurity. But when the upstart is a female it simply adds insult to injury. Not only is their status as executives threatened but their status as males, and heaven help the unfortunate woman who dares to challenge that.

These classic bureaucrats should not be underestimated. They may appear to be a bit of a joke but their power to put obstacles in your path is quite considerable. Firstly they have the 'system' on their side.

The 'system' acts rather like the House of Lords does on the Commons, as a sort of brake on the wilder excesses of company whizz-kids who want everything to happen at once. Eventually the whizz-kids will triumph, if their aims are plainly the right ones, but the bureaucrats with the aid of the 'system' will hold them up as long as they possibly can, often mounting the most ridiculous last ditch stand in a battle they know they cannot win.

These conflicts usually rage well below the level of top management. The distant sound of battle may be heard in the boardroom, but the directors are concerned with more important matters. They are usually quite content to let the lower orders fight it out and let the best man or woman win.

Bearing all this in mind, it is fairly obvious that the bureaucrats will be on the watch, charting your every move. Have you sneaked an illicit coffee machine into the building? Have you been buying ashtrays for your office out of the petty cash? Have you been ordering mini cabs without signed authority? Or getting hold of stationery without filling in the proper forms?

These things have been noted and will be held in evidence. Do not be surprised if all sorts of inexplicable blockages and obstacles start to appear.

Do you need a new telephone? There may be mysterious delays and evasive answers. Your request for an extra chair for visitors will be refused for no obvious reason. Your expenses will be queried by some distant personage in the finance department. Your intended trip abroad, which to you appears amply justified, may be delayed by some trifling hold-up in the travel department. A most unpleasant memo with a copy to the head of your department may suddenly appear, accusing you of smuggling gin into the building.

It will pay you to take heed of these warnings. You may

suddenly be required to justify some of your apparently innocent actions, and at a level which will surprise you.

It will not take long to discover who these hidden enemies are. A few enquiries will soon reveal where the 'Pockets of Resistance' are located, and once having discovered them your tactics should be carefully planned.

The first rule is NEVER ATTACK A POCKET OF RESISTANCE HEAD ON.

He has read the small print, he knows all the rules. He has got the system on his side and he is determined to use it, so you can't win by direct methods.

Something more subtle is required. Be prepared for a long siege. The Pockets are well entrenched and it is up to you to outwit them and eventually if possible bring them round to your side.

The first aim is to allay their feelings of insecurity. How can they possibly think of Little You as any sort of threat? To soothe their hurt feelings you must set out at once to make them feel important. Apologize for your transgressions and explain you acted in ignorance. Consult them on all sorts of matters however trivial. Keep asking them their advice. Hint that you rely strongly on their experience and wisdom in everything you do. Encourage them to talk about themselves and their careers, their past triumphs and victories.

Try to remember their birthdays and wish them many happy returns. But don't overdo it. You don't want them to become suspicious. Move slowly, or you will startle your quarry into instant retreat. Rather like stalking a rare and timid animal, you must proceed with extreme caution.

Very few men can resist this sort of treatment. If it works, they will soon cease to regard you as an adversary and will begin to look on you as a disciple to whom they are giving the benefit of their knowledge. Even eventually as a friend. Limited though these bureaucrats may be in their outlook, they can be quite interesting about things like the company's history, and you may grow almost fond of them in time.

However cleverly you work at winning these gentlemen over, you may still find one or two Pockets of Resistance who are impervious to your blandishments. There is only one course of action open to you, and that is to 'work around' them.

'Successful management is to do with people and chemistry' is a favourite saying of captains of industry. Don't scoff, there's a lot in it.

The reason why your Pocket of Resistance is so intractable may be because the chemistry is wrong. If you sense an implacable hostility, don't ignore the signs.

The eyes are the key.

If the P of R declines to look you in the eye, or if his eyes go blank when he does, you know that you are up against a Super-Pocket.

Most human beings manage to establish some sort of rapport given time, but if this particular Pocket continues to give you the eye treatment indefinitely, you will have to admit defeat.

Do it with a good grace and don't keep on trying when you know it won't work. It will just become embarrassing for both of you.

In future take care never to sit down next to him in the executive restaurant, or speak to him in the lift unless you are spoken to. It is far better to adopt his own tactics towards you and pretend that he doesn't exist.

It is possible that after many months or even years the Super-Pocket may at last accept the fact that you have been a good loser and give you a wintry smile. But don't bank on it.

Having lost this particular battle, you now have to by-pass. In the Middle Ages, if a castle under siege held out too long, the attackers sometimes got bored and just went round it, hoping the besieged were too exhausted to dash out later and stab them in the back. This is a risk you have to take.

If dealings with a Super-Pocket are unavoidable, never go to him direct. By the laws of middle management hierarchy he will certainly have an executive above him to whom he reports and probably a deputy or assistant, plus a secretary, below him.

If protocol dictates that some decision or other has to go through the Super-Pocket's department, either try and go to the man above him, if the matter is of sufficient importance, or to the man below, who will be empowered to act on his behalf in less weighty matters.

If something just needs to be signed, make sure you've gone through all the proper procedures and then if necessary get his secretary to ask the Super-Pocket to sign it.

Try and do as much business as possible with the Super-Pocket's department when he is away or on holiday, so as to keep contact with him to the minimum.

Keep a low profile when he is around. Do as little as you can to attract his attention, and you will find his power to obstruct you drastically reduced.

Even so it is not safe to relax. A Super-Pocket will always be lying in wait to trap the unwary. So make sure that all your dealings with him and his department are meticulously carried out according to the letter of the law. It may be a bore, but you become neglectful at your peril.

One note of consolation. The truth is that deep down the Super-Pocket is almost certainly more scared than you are.

Guide to Pocket Spotting - an Early Warning System

Spotting possible trouble-making Pockets early on gives you a chance to avoid aggravation later. There are certain signs to look for.

Closed Doors

Anybody who habitually keeps his office door shut is suspect, because closed doors can mean a closed mind. What has he got to hide? Or is he trying to shut out the world?

Pipes

The smoking of pipes is often associated with old-fashioned 'masculine' values – solidity, paternalism, support for the establishment. It's all pretty bad news.

Short Hair

This can be deceptive. Short back-and-sides is sometimes adopted by fashionable young men. But if the man is over forty, watch out.

Tidiness

Obsessive tidiness in the office is a bad sign. It means the occupant doesn't want things disturbed. It may also mean he is insecure. Either way it is a danger signal.

Hours

Anybody who arrives and leaves the office at exactly the same time every day is really set in his ways. Proceed with caution.

Cars

Obsessive car cleaning is quite definitely something to be concerned about. If the car he is polishing is not even his own but belongs to the company, he may snap at any minute.

Appearance

A man who appears unnaturally clean and well-pressed is also worth investigating. He may be an ex-army officer (not a good sign). He may prove to be homosexual, which is quite another story. (See page 44.)

Pens in the Pocket

Ball-point pens in the Pocket's pocket are the outward and visible sign of a bureaucratic mind.

Moustaches

There are two main types of these, the 'toothbrush' (bad) or the 'bandit' (all right).

Beards

Men with beards usually seem to be trying to create either an 'artistic' or 'sea-dog' effect. They may actually turn out to be painters, writers or sailors – or actors playing a 'character' part.

There aren't many bewhiskered businessmen about, but should you come across one, he will almost certainly turn out to be harmless.

Conclusion

An over forty, short-haired, pipe-smoking, door-closing, car-cleaning, punctual, tidy man with an open mind on the subject of female executives may exist, but he is as rare as a tortoiseshell tom cat.

Other Women

As we have already established, women can be friends. But it is a sad fact that women are brought up to distrust each other and this may be the automatic reaction of some other females in the company. They may feel jealous of your success and resent the way you are muscling in on the territory over which they have reigned as sole female for so long. This is a very small-minded old-fashioned attitude but unfortunately it does occur among some less enlightened members of your own sex.

If the female is well established in the department into which you have been promoted she probably looks upon the male executives as her private property, and suspects that you may be about to woo them away from her influence. This kind of woman executive is probably either unmarried or unhappily so, and depends on the men around her to flirt with her and boost her morale. A perfectly understandable and blameless situation.

You must immediately calm her fears by making it quite clear that you have absolutely no designs on any of the males in the department, and that you are just there to do your job to the best of your ability.

Women being on the whole reasonable creatures, she will soon realize that you will be more use as an ally than an enemy, but it may take time. Try and keep away from any males of whom she seems particularly possessive and approach her in a friendly woman to woman way, asking her advice and getting on as friendly terms with her as she will permit.

In the unlikely event of her turning out to be another Super-Pocket it will almost certainly be the old trouble of complete lack of rapport or a gulf in views about basic matters, like politics or life in general, so wide that it cannot be bridged.

If she is sensible she will probably conclude that she will be the loser if she fails to meet your friendly overtures and that she needs you more than vice versa. The fact is that men being as they are she will probably get little support from them in an all-out war. Men have little patience with what they regard as female squabbles and will soon decide that she is behaving in a thoroughly neurotic and silly way. This unfortunate situation is to be avoided if possible, but it may be inevitable.

If it happens, try to treat your vanquished enemy with as much kindness and consideration as you can. She may never be your friend, but at least give her as little cause as possible to dislike you.

Even further down the scale you may come across some really bolshie young female who decides to challenge your authority. She believes she is every bit as good as you are, so don't go giving yourself airs as if you were her superior. Men can get away with it but not you.

If you are giving yourself airs, it is as well to stop it at once, whoever you may be dealing with, but the way to placate this cocky young woman is to make her laugh. She is probably trying it on to see how far she can go with you, calling you by your christian name uninvited and making it quite clear you had better not try to pull any rank on her.

Make her realize that you regard the whole thing as a joke just as much as she does. Treat her familiarity as perfectly natural between females in a man's world. But give as good as you get.

You may feel it's hardly worth bothering with someone so

obviously beneath your notice. It is. This girl is testing you as a female executive. You may be the first one she has ever come across. It is up to you to gain her respect, if only to persuade her that you're not some sort of freak. Next time she comes across a woman in an executive position, she will be that much more likely to accept her as part of the normal office scene.

The fact that she singled you out as a target may mean that she has got potential herself and is wondering how she would cope in your position. Without sounding too pompous, you are actually setting her some sort of example.

As well as the odd female executive who may cause trouble, there may also be women further down the scale who look on you with disfavour. Sometimes a very long-serving secretary, perhaps to some fairly high-placed executive, will view your progress with a jaundiced eye. It is only to be expected.

She may have been with the company for twenty-five years without progressing one inch beyond her secretarial status. It is only natural that she will have mixed feelings about someone who has managed to break out of the mould and achieve something she has failed to do – reach executive level.

To understand all is to forgive all and it is up to you to make it clear that you respect her position in the company and that you are sympathetic to her view that she could have done just as well as you have, given the chance.

When what appears to be pointless malice on her part is revealed as a perfectly natural envy of your success, you can afford to be magnanimous. She is really paying you a compliment. Let her unburden herself to you and you will find that she's simply hurt that her talents have gone so unappreciated all these years. There but for the Grace of God go you, so be understanding and try to make her last years with the company as pleasant as possible. As one of the casualties of the 'system', she deserves your support.

6
Umbrella Time

There was an old man of Thermopylae
Who never did anything properly
Edward Lear 1812–1888

Great men are not always wise.
Job 32:9

Your umbrella should of course be at the ready at all times, but there will be certain occasions during your business life when it is particularly essential to be prepared, and put your umbrella up well in advance.

Most of these are classic situations in which we all find ourselves sooner or later, and the vast majority pass off without mishap. They are, however, fraught with danger.

Many an innocent party has come unstuck through not taking note of the thin ice on which they are skating at some critical point in their career. The most potentially dangerous period for you is

When the Boss is on Holiday

Robert Townsend in his book *Up the Organization*, raises this thorny problem of what happens when the boss is abroad or on holiday.

Townsend is against the appointing of a deputy on the grounds that by doing so, the boss is obliged publicly to appear to be appointing his successor, which he may not be ready, or willing, to do.

A boss has another incentive for going away and leaving no one in charge.

It is to his advantage in maintaining the principle of 'divide and rule'.

If the various people in the department are unsure which, if any of them, is actually supposed to be the senior, they will all work harder (so the theory goes) to prove how efficient and responsible they can be in the boss's absence.

The system is not so likely to come unstuck in a small organization where everyone knows everyone else and the communications are good. If the other people in the building have all been there for some time and know from way back exactly who in your department does what, it may well be okay for the boss to depart with an easy mind.

In a company which is large or where the communications are bad the disadvantages of the system soon become evident.

If there is a high turnover of staff in the company, or even worse if there is a new chairman or managing director who has just taken over, isn't too familiar with the ropes and doesn't know who is the right person to advise on some important decision, disaster may well lie ahead.

The head of your department, if he has any sense at all, will at least leave a phone number with his headless department in case of emergency. But, amazingly enough, this doesn't always happen.

It is up to you in this situation to be on your guard.

One of your colleagues may well take the opportunity of the boss's absence to start throwing his weight about and even giving you orders.

(Sometimes just to make things even more confusing, the boss will privately tell one of his staff that he is leaving him in charge, without telling anyone else. This isn't fair on anyone, but it *does* happen.)

Unless he has been publicly designated as the boss's deputy by the boss himself, you will need to employ a great deal of tact and diplomacy to put this upstart politely in his place. It is essential that he gets the message early on that just because you are female, you are not prepared to be put upon.

In these days of airline strikes and extreme weather conditions, it sometimes happens that the boss is *unexpectedly* marooned abroad and you may find yourself up against the problem of the Paranoid Status Seeker.

The PSS's obsession, for that is what it is, is to step into the boss's shoes.

If by some unfortunate circumstance the PSS answers the phone when the boss rings to explain that he is stuck in Milan or wherever and will everyone please carry on as best they can, the PSS will at once assume that he has been put in charge.

To him a nod is as good as a wink and he will conclude that his wishful thinking has become fact.

On the principle that Nature abhors a vacuum, the PSS's Pavlovian reaction is to fill this sudden gap and he will automatically start moving into the boss's office.

Should anyone raise an eyebrow, he will be quick to explain that he has some complicated work to do and it's quieter in there; or that there's an important Transatlantic call coming through on the boss's line and he might as well take it at the boss's desk.

The PSS will hang around the boss's secretary, making remarks like 'If there's anything urgent in the mail, just give it to me and I'll deal with it.'

He will start putting his car in the boss's parking space, without permission, and will let it be known to members of the board that in the boss's absence, he (the PSS) is on call if required.

The PSS is really less of a threat than a nuisance, as long as you have a tough and dominant boss who will reassert himself as soon as he gets back, put a stop to all this nonsense and make it clear who is in charge.

The PSS will quickly retreat and the *status quo* will be restored.

If your boss is an innocent weakling it is up to you (should he deserve such loyalty) to drop a word of warning about this take-over bid.

He may be quite unaware that there is a cuckoo in his nest. In nature, the cuckoo always wins, but only because the other birds are too small or too stupid to resist.

During any period while the boss is away a real emergency may develop in which advice over an important financial or policy issue has to be given, or a fast vital decision has to be made by someone in your department.

This situation can be potentially highly dangerous.

You may opt for ducking out of it and leaving your colleagues to stick their necks out, which being men, they will probably be quite eager and willing to do.

The safest thing is to make up your own mind what you think the answer is and then wait to be asked.

Because you are a woman, you almost certainly won't be.

If the others have made the wrong decision, there will be a *post mortem* when the boss gets back. You will then be in the clear. All you have to say is 'Well, nobody asked me.' Smug, but true. If you are sure you are right and the others wrong, you can give your decision, preferably in front of witnesses. Here at last is your chance to shine.

If your advice isn't followed, come the *post mortem*, you can say 'I gave them my advice but unfortunately they didn't take it.'

However disastrous for the company the consequences of this mix-up may be, it is quite possible that no one will actually be fired.

After a few recriminations and nasty scenes with everyone accusing everyone else, the whole thing will be put down to the unfortunate fact that the crisis occurred while the boss was away, so no one (including him) is really to blame.

Some years ago, a friend of mine found herself involved on the fringe of just such a débâcle. Her boss, who had gone off on a motoring holiday leaving no address and no deputy, returned to find his department in a state of disarray after a major error of judgement by one of his staff – an overconfident young man who had not been with them long.

At her boss's request, my friend explained what had happened, ending with the words, 'If you don't mind my saying so, I think the mistake you made was . . .'

'I DO NOT MAKE MISTAKES !' he interrupted sternly, thus putting an end to the conversation.

It is a classic example of what I can only call Masculine Logic.

This is an extremely complex and, at first sight, highly improbable method of arriving at a given conclusion. You may never actually comprehend it, but you will have to learn to live with it if you are to survive in business.

The basic fact to grasp is that, contrary to common belief, men do not run their businesses in a rational manner.

At first it may be hard to accept the evidence of your own eyes that this is so. Some women never seem able to achieve this acceptance and live in a constant and futile state of amazement at what they see going on around them.

A perfectly intelligent female executive of my acquaintance, even after several years in business, still used to say to me 'But how can they do it?' over some piece of masculine folly which was inevitably going to land the man concerned in a perfectly foreseeable catastrophe.

'Surely by now,' I would say, 'you have given up expecting sensible decisions from these blokes.'

Their actions appear to be based on entirely other considerations. What these considerations are, is beyond the scope of a lay person to explain and beyond the scope of this book. They probably lie deep in the male psyche, and are unconscious throwbacks to the time when men lived in caves and hunted in packs.

Having made a close study of male executives in action over a number of years, I am convinced that the roots of their behaviour do indeed lie somewhere far back in pre-history, and that their conduct is often governed more by emotional ('seat-of-the-pants') reactions and instincts of aggression and confrontation than by purely rational thought.

These theories are not of course new. We may never know the truth, or at least not in our lifetime.

Perhaps the whole thing is best summed up in the laconic (and totally unhelpful) old western phrase 'A man's got to do what a man's got to do.'

Nothing Succeeds Like Failure

Another manifestation of the strange workings of Masculine Logic is the 'nothing succeeds like failure' syndrome.

A small mistake will probably be ignored by the bosses.

Several trifling mistakes in a row may cause them some irritation and even result in the executive being asked to leave.

A really spectacular mistake, however, costing the company several million pounds, may result in the man concerned actually being promoted.

This seems so unlikely that even the wilder excesses of Masculine Logic can hardly explain it. But I can assure you that there are well-documented examples of this happening, and in large, established, reputable companies to boot.

If men are really so incompetent and so swayed by primitive emotions, how is it that the wheels of commerce continue to turn? Why doesn't the whole economy grind to a halt?

After reading behind-the-scenes accounts of what went on at the highest levels before and during the last two world wars, one might equally wonder how we managed to win them. The answer must be that the enemy commanders were even sillier than ours. Or luck was on our side. Times haven't changed. Nowadays it is still touch and go, but somehow we manage to muddle through – just like in the war.

Men have simply transferred their war games from the battlefield to the boardroom.

Having accepted these strange facts of masculine life, you would be well advised to abandon the fruitless quest for what makes men tick and get on with the job in hand – advancing your own career.

7
The Status Game

> Naught venture, naught gain.
> *Thomas Tusser (1524–80)*

As we have already agreed, the chances are that you are more intelligent than your colleagues. Therefore it will soon be obvious that you should be given a more senior position.

But even after proving your superior efficiency, you are still at the bottom of the heap, the most junior of the team. Some departments go in for organization charts which will confirm the fact. But some of these charts are so cunningly devised that it is impossible to be sure.

If you have any doubts about your position, look at the arrangement of names in each department as listed in the company telephone directory. This is a give-away document. There, at least in a company of any size, will be listed names in order of seniority. The head of the department's name at the top and so on down. If after a certain level, such as the deputy, if there is one, the names are not in alphabetical order, you can be pretty sure they are in order of seniority and that means status. If you are at the bottom of the pile, your first efforts must be directed to changing the situation.

Before you can increase your status in the company, however, you must learn how to play the status game.

The first thing to look for in any campaign is the enemy's weakness. It won't take you long to discover that status is the businessman's Achilles Heel.

Once launched on the status war, there are no chivalric or Geneva Conventions to restrain the warriors. All too soon they will descend to spreading scandal and gossip about their colleagues.

Men can be unbelievably vicious about each other, and the

sort of backbiting that reputedly goes on at women's coffee parties is like the cooing of doves compared with the slurs cast by businessmen on the honesty, sanity and even virility of their rivals.

Nothing is sacred in the status war.

So here you are with a big advantage. You don't really care a fig about status.

You are merely in it for the money and the satisfaction of doing a good job.

While the dinosaurs **are** battling it out overhead, you sit tight.

Those who don't succumb to ulcers or nervous breakdowns may well destroy each other, which can only be to the good as far as you're concerned.

Most male executives are so obsessively involved in trying to upstage each other in the battle for status, that it is not surprising that they feel quite worn out at the end of the day and when they get home can only flop into a chair saying they've had a terrible day at the office. Their wives, of course, are under the impression that they are suffering from overwork.

There is no doubt that if all the energy expended by businessmen in this internecine warfare was channelled into increasing productivity, all Britain's economic problems would be solved overnight.

The more insecure a man feels, the more he will cling to his status symbols. They are his reassurance that he is needed. They are bulwarks against what he sees as the encroaching hordes of upstarts, male and female, who think they can cut through the red tape and go places.

The older of these insecure characters expect to be treated with the respect due to their age and experience. They tend to be hedged about with status – giving senior secretaries and personal assistants to keep the world at bay. Inaccessibility is their weapon. They are always in meetings or 'unavailable' for some other reason. These gentlemen are usually bogged down in a morass of largely superfluous paperwork.

Many of them are elaborate frauds. Behind those large cars,

chauffeurs, assistants, secretaries, big desks and batteries of telephones there is a human being.

By the time he has acquired all these perks, he's probably a
nice old gentleman who simply wants to be protected from the
irritations of everyday existence.

It's not a bad life, and if you want to share it, you will have
to play the status game. But first, to recognize the symbols.

Some are more recognizable than others. Some are so secret
that only the company secretary and the board of directors are
privy to the names of those who enjoy them.

Here is a guide to some status symbols and their significance.

The Office

The size and location of your office is of course the most obvious
indicator of your position in the company. As a rule spaciousness
(or lack of it) is the key.

From all accounts this obsession with office size once reached
its peak at Fords, where I am told every inch of floor space and
centimetre of carpet, even every pot plant, had its significance.

Provided he has a tape measure, nobody in a company like
that need have any doubt about where he stands on the ladder.

This sort of thing obviously has its advantages – everybody
knows exactly where they are in relation to everybody else. But
it is by no means common.

Office Décor

Standard company furniture will be your lot until you get to the
level of choosing your own. When the time comes, try to avoid
the unfortunate lapses of your male colleagues, who usually end
up with huge square leather sofas, smacking more of the airport
lounge than the executive suite.

If you can also select the colour of your walls and carpets, you
really have arrived.

Doors

No door to your office is bad. A door with a glass panel through which you may be observed by passers-by is not much better. Frosted glass is a compromise. A good solid door is the thing to aim for.

Telephones

More than two telephones is pure ostentation and will impress nobody. Any *one* gadget which involves pressing buttons is an acceptable perk. It implies that you deal with such urgent business that you need a hot-line to contact other top executives.

Secretaries

A secretary can hardly be regarded as a status symbol. She is accepted as a necessity by most executives even at the lowliest levels. Two secretaries, on the other hand, are certainly an indication that their boss is so busy that he must be pretty important. But this depends on the kind of job he is doing. If he is the managing director of a subsidiary or head of a large division, for instance, he may only have one secretary, but that is because he has a large number of executives under him, all with their own secretaries, who are carrying out the work for him.

A large number of assistants and secretaries may merely indicate that you have a lot of work dumped on you. It doesn't necessarily mean that you have a lot of power or that you have a very high status.

Typewriters

If you started as a secretary yourself you are one of the cognoscenti who can spot the make of typewriter a secretary is using and draw your own conclusions. In most large companies the kind of typewriter a secretary may choose is laid down – ranging from the lowliest Olympia to the highest IBM – according to the status of her boss.

Tea and Coffee on a Tray

This is another office status symbol. It means that your secretary doesn't present your coffee to you in a paper cup from the coffee machine, or from the trolley which comes round the office at a specified time.

It means that a tray with actual china – a tea (or coffee) pot, cups, saucers, milk, sugar and even biscuits – will be brought to your office by a waitress.

If you have any sense you will arrange for your preferred blend of coffee to be made in your office.

The Company Car

A company car, like a secretary, is not much of a status symbol. Everybody who is anybody has one, because it is one of the ways a company can compensate a man for not paying him a higher salary. (As my company car wasn't really essential, I asked if I could give it up and have some more money instead. The answer was in the negative.) Private insurance schemes also come into this category.

But cars can give away the *level* which an executive has reached. It is an outward and visible sign for all to see.

A straightforward basic mass-produced model with no frills such as a cassette player, sunshine roof or fog-lamps, indicates that the owner is probably a run-of-the-mill salesman or a junior executive of a fairly low grade.

The optional extras are the signs to look for these days.

The reason for this is the fashion for top executives to keep a low profile, because of the threat of kidnapping, or to set a good example in energy conservation, or just because conspicuous consumption is out of date.

All this has made car-spotting more difficult.

It is not so much the type of car as the extras which give the game away. Though there are certain cars which can give you a clue.

Rolls Royces

These are now entirely *déclassé*, considered vulgarly ostentatious and only suitable for rock stars, their managers, showbiz tycoons or foreign royalty, who are presumed not to know any better.

This is a pity, because they are extremely attractive and comfortable cars, but such is the fickleness of fashion.

Mercedes

Energy conservationists have taken their toll of all such formerly desirable vehicles, but a *small* Mercedes is acceptable, though only as a second car for a wife or favoured offspring. It is unlikely to be seen in the company garage.

Jaguars, Rovers, Ford Granadas and their Variations

These seem to be the current favourites among top industrialists, giving the right sort of down-to-earth image, while allowing for plenty of leg-room, and all sorts of extras, like special fuel-saving engines, electrically operated windows and all the refinements such as quadraphonic sound to which such VIPs are accustomed.

Minis

Minis are often employed by top people to ferry them around big cities with the minimum of delay. A highly polished, chauffeur-driven Mini with expensive trimmings or any other indication of personalized treatment almost certainly contains a personage rich in status.

Chauffeurs

My idea of the ultimate perk is a car (I'm not fussy about the make) with a driver permanently at my disposal, getting from A to B at the fastest possible speed being to me the height of luxury.

A personal chauffeur is undoubtedly a status symbol devoutly to be wished for, but you will have to get very high indeed before the company decides that you are really worth it.

Senior executives who are not on chauffeur level are in the habit of hiring chauffeur-driven cars to drive them around. It has been estimated that the amount of money spent on these hired cars far exceeds the sum which would be needed to pay a number of extra staff chauffeurs who could be on call for managers of a certain level.

This constitutes another interesting example of the workings of Masculine Logic.

First Class Air Travel

It is quite likely that a junior executive will be prepared to fork out extra cash to install a tape-player, radio or other refinement in his basic company car. To a casual observer this can give the impression that the owner of the car is more prestigious than he really is.

To pay the difference between a tourist and first-class air ticket is quite another matter for anyone who does much travelling.

Only the most status-crazed of individuals would consider embarking on such a costly exercise.

In any case the staff of the company travel office whose job it is to book the tickets would almost certainly blow the gaff and disseminate the news of any such extravagantly eccentric behaviour, thus defeating the object of the exercise.

The privilege of flying everywhere first class at the company's expense is therefore a copper-bottomed status symbol unmatched in prestige by almost any other.

It also gives rise to more resentment, bad feeling and aggravation, perhaps for the reasons explained above.

You can't hide the fact that the company views you as a second-rate traveller, nor can you fake the fact that they think that you are absolutely first class.

Invitation to the Company Dinner

This can vary in prestige from one organization to another. It all depends where the 'cut-off' line is drawn.

If the affair is very large and includes junior executives and their wives, you can forget about it as a status occasion.

If it is a more exclusive party, it is fascinating to work out who is who in the company by watching to see who is smuggling a dinner jacket into the office on the morning of the event. It is certainly worth working late to observe which wives are arriving in the office in long dresses to rendezvous with their husbands before proceeding by taxi mini cab or chauffeur driven company car (according of course to status) to this exclusive annual event.

The chosen few do not bother to make much of a secret of the fact that they have been bidden to the Ball, and you can be sure that there will be plenty of envious Cinderellas brooding bitterly over their exclusion.

Ironically the people who are on this privileged list are probably the ones who are likely to enjoy the evening least and look on it as more of a duty than a pleasure.

One must sometimes suffer to be important, and it is worth remembering that a high rate of attendance at tedious functions is one of the penalties of the over-statused executive.

The Company Flat

This, like first-class air travel, is a gold-plated perk for top people. But it is not entirely fake-proof.

It is possible for a well-heeled executive with a private income or a rich spouse to treat himself to a *pied-à-terre*, while hinting that the company is paying the rent or at least contributing to it.

Unlike the first-class perk, therefore, the metropolitan flat is not a reliable status-indicator.

Serious symbol-spotters should treat it with due caution.

The Title Game

Titles are important status symbols and businessmen are excessively title-conscious. They will fight tooth and nail for the right to call themselves 'Chairman', 'Managing Director' or 'Director'.

If you work for a big group with a number of divisions and subsidiaries, you can have a lot of fun watching the Title Game.

Suppose your employer is the famous MCP group of companies, and Joe Bloggs is in charge of a subsidiary. He will persuade his superiors to let him describe himself as 'Chairman and Managing Director, MCP Cereals and Cornflakes Division Ltd'.

Joe Bloggs is no fool. He knows that nobody in their right mind is going to remember a title like that. It will inevitably be *shortened*. When Joe Bloggs gets interviewed, or quoted in the press, he knows perfectly well that the first thing the 'subs' will do is chop out all this nonsense about cornflakes. In the morning he will find himself described in the paper as 'Joe Bloggs, Chairman of MCP'.

Nobody inside the company will be taken in for an instant, but the question will be posed in their minds: Could Joe Bloggs ever actually make Group Chairman? Is this a portent?

Outsiders, including of course the Bloggs' neighbours and acquaintances, who have only the haziest idea who MCP's Chairman actually is, will be suitably impressed. Joe Bloggs will apologize profusely to his superiors, quite legitimately blaming the newspaper for the mistake. But somehow he'll never actually get round to demanding a correction.

The Key to the Executive Loo

As a woman you can almost certainly forget about this one.

No company is likely to allocate a special loo to one woman or even two or three. So until unisex loos arrive on the scene, you will have to continue to do the democratic thing along with your secretarial sisters.

The Anti-Status Phenomenon

One of the most powerful and successful men I ever met not only worked from a pokey office, but declared that he didn't require a secretary. He even left his office door wide open so that anyone could stroll in and out.

He went on to become head of one of the company's largest divisions and he's still on his way up.

This kind of one-upmanship, which includes coming to work on a bike and eating sandwiches in the office for lunch, is only recommended for those rare beings with absolute confidence in their own ability and no doubts whatever about their future.

Extreme status-consciousness in any individual is a sign of weakness and those suffering from it are unlikely to be found at the top of the company, or headed that way. As a general rule, therefore, the less important an executive is, the more status-conscious he is likely to be and therefore the more respectfully you should treat him.

Those with real power are usually impatient of too much deference and prefer to cut the niceties and get quickly to the point.

They appreciate straight talk, if it is intelligent, constructive and relevant.

Very few people are prepared to talk 'man to man' with the boss.

He is surrounded by yes-men, fearful for their jobs. You as a woman, i.e. having nothing much to lose, may speak bluntly, and ninety-nine times out of a hundred your frankness will be welcomed.

A Final Note of Warning

Although it is important to monitor your progress, or lack of it, in the company, you should not make the mistake of your male colleagues and get too status-conscious.

By all means keep tabs on your position, but don't let it become an obsession.

Status-chasing should never become an end in itself.

For many people, getting bogged down in the means has proved to be the beginning of the end.

8
The Male Put-down and How To Counter It

> And as she look'd about, she did behold,
> How over that same door was likewise writ
> 'Be bold, be bold and everywhere be bold.'
> *Edmund Spenser (1552–99)*

Men, like most male animals, have a number of ploys which they use to put down their inferiors and exact homage from them.

The male stickleback, for example, darkens with rage and stands on his head in the water.

The hairy-nosed wombat bares his teeth and tosses his head.

The mongoose wrinkles his nose and gives a loud screech, and those animals (like hamsters) who are lucky enough to have them, can indulge in 'cheek-pouch inflation' which produces an effect 'both disconcerting and daunting'.*

The dominant male in a group of animals will thus display his mastery over the others by challenging them to defy his authority and then making them back down.

Men also need this constant reassurance that they are still in charge. When dealing with women, their tactics are slightly different from those they employ against members of their own sex.

The 'I am an older, wiser, stronger and therefore superior being' approach will be used on both sexes, but with women an even more patronizing line can be taken.

There is a wide range of gambits to keep you in your place. Some of the most popular are:

The Protection Racket

The 'I'm only trying to protect you' line is illustrated as follows. If your boss feels you are getting slightly 'uppity' and out of

*Marler and Hamilton, *Mechanism of Animal Behaviour* (Wiley, 1966) and Ewer, *Ethology of Mammals* (Elek, 1973).

control, he may decide to have a little talk with you which goes something like this:

'Now, Veronica, I know you've made all the arrangements for the conference next Thursday but I think I should point out that you may get criticism about the actual venue you have chosen. Have you ensured that all the microphones are working/the fire regulations have been adhered to/there is somewhere for the directors to park their cars? *I am only trying* to *protect you* by pointing out these matters which you may have overlooked.'

The words 'I'm only trying to protect you' are the key to the whole business.

They are designed to make you feel insecure and doubtful about your ability to arrange a conference, to undermine your self-confidence. (They also cover your boss should things go wrong. 'Oh well,' he can say afterwards, 'I did try to warn the poor girl. Maybe she's trying to bite off more than she can chew.')

Your boss's implication in all this is that you are a bit of a flibberty-gibbet likely to land in hot water unless restrained by wiser counsel. What he is saying, ever so obliquely, is 'I'm cleverer than you are, so watch your step.'

This kind of thing can be quite unnerving, but keep your head and thank him politely for his concern – after all, his threats are merely bluff, a try-on to make you acknowledge who is master.

If you are satisfied that you have done everything possible to make the conference a success, then you can do no more. Relax, and above all don't panic.

Don't play into his hands by rushing about spreading alarm and despondency among your own staff.

Panic is catching and all your carefully thought-out arrangements may be jeopardized if you start trying to alter or improve on them at the last minute.

The 'Olde Worlde Courtesie' Line

I believe it was the troubadours in the Middle Ages who started all this nonsense of **putting** women on pedestals, 'looking up to them' and treating them with exaggerated courtesy.

They called their new invention 'chivalry' and it gave men the pretext for all sorts of diabolical behaviour, like locking up women in chastity belts (to preserve their virtue) and marooning them in remote towers (for safety), thus allowing them to be captured by villains, so that chivalrous knights could rescue them and cover themselves with glory.

The aim of chivalry was to flatter women into believing that all this 'respectful' treatment was for their own good.

The real idea was to get the women out of the way or into a subservient role and keep them there, thus freeing the men to get on with the proper business of life at the time – i.e. war, murder, pillage, rape, etc. – unrestrained by interfering wives and girl friends.

The whole thing was a big con, an elaborate put-down on a massive scale, and it's still going on today, right here in the office.

The 'good manners' ploy can take all sorts of seemingly innocent guises.

Look out for exaggeratedly old-fashioned forms of politeness.

If a man opens a door, bows deeply and says, 'After you, dear lady', or makes a special point of walking on the outside of the pavement, he should go at once on to the 'suspected Pocket of Resistance' list.

A lot of men, particularly the older ones, carry out all these actions quite naturally as a result of early conditioning, but once such behaviour becomes exaggerated, be warned.

The simplest way of dealing with the door-opening ploy is to hold the door for *him* and say, 'You don't need to do that any more now, you know!'

This may irritate him into assuming that you are a rabid feminist, but the point will be taken.

The 'No Swearing in Front of Ladies' Ploy

The whole object of the Olde Worlde Courtesie line is to cause you to feel excluded from the male group, and one of the favourite ploys to make you uncomfortable and *de trop* in masculine company, is to use a four-letter word and then apologize profusely, inferring that 'Ladies' (a favourite pseudo-chivalric word) have no idea what these words mean and would be horrified if they did.

Like 'Not in front of the children', 'Not in front of the ladies', implies that you are overhearing conversation normally reserved for a superior group, in this case, men.

Countering the 'no swearing' attack (for that is what it is) is difficult.

You can let drop a few four-letter words yourself. But this will only give your colleagues the idea that you are used to mixing with low company, not good for the image.

'What makes you think I'm that ladylike?' is probably as good a retort as any.

The whispered telling of dirty jokes is another way in which men 'gang up' on females in their midst.

As ninety-nine per cent of dirty jokes are jokes against women, this form of teasing is nasty enough to be taken as an affront to your dignity, and should be treated as such. Should you be naive enough to ask what all the sniggering is about, you will be told 'Not for the ears of *Ladies*' or some such fatuous remark.

The dirty joke ploy, like the 'Girlie' Calendar ploy (see next section), is only normally used by the more moronic gentlemen in your office, or perhaps by those too young to know better.

To ignore them and avoid their company is probably the most advisable course of action for you to take.

The 'Girlie' Calendar Ploy

A ploy sometimes used by a man who feels threatened is to hang a 'girlie' calendar in a conspicuous position in his office, where you can't help seeing it. This seemingly innocent act is a sign that the man concerned is trying to tell you something about yourself in order to undermine your self-confidence.

Under the pretence of 'admiring' women, this man is actually giving you a back-handed compliment.

Let me explain.

These calendars specialize in showing naked girls in acrobatic and usually humiliating poses, and the idea is to cut you down to size and remind you of your proper role in life as a sex-object.

Not only that, the pictures of these slim, young, glamorous women are intended to rub your nose in the fact that, even as a sex-object, you don't measure up. *Your* slimness, youth and glamour relegate you firmly to the second eleven; you may even qualify as a non-starter.

Though the 'girlie' calendar ploy is only ever used by the least intelligent and sophisticated of your work-mates, it is none the less irritating for that.

The obvious counter is to obtain one of the few male sex-object calendars on the market and hang it in your office.

Failing that, cut out some coloured photographs from *Play Girl* and have them tastefully framed for your office wall.

Unfortunately, few women have the necessary courage to take logical countermeasures. Most of us are far too lily-livered to carry retaliation boldly into the enemy camp.

As an alternative you could slap an 'Exploits Women' sticker on the offending picture, but this involves invading the owner's territory and violating his property, always a highly provocative act, which could result in hostilities escalating out of control.

For the faint-hearted, the best way out is to avoid the offender's office, or if you have to enter it, ignore the whole thing. This negative strategy may, in the long run, actually prove the most effective.

The 'Cold Shoulder' Line

This takes various forms, from habitually sending you memos signed 'on behalf of Joe Bloggs in his absence', to allowing the lift doors to close just as you are approaching them.

A fairly common tactic, among more junior executives, is to leave you out of the party making its ritual visit to the pub at lunch-time. This has the effect of isolating you from the herd, and ensuring that you are in no doubt about your exclusion from the male-bond group, in spite of the fact that you all work together as a team in the office.

This psychological warfare should not worry you unduly. It is true that you may miss out on some of the latest company gossip, but you have your own spy network to rely on in this respect.

Console yourself with the reflection that by spending their lunch hours in smoky pubs eating stale pork pies and drinking fizzy beer they are laying the foundations of the paunches, heart disease and bronchitis which will certainly afflict, or even kill them off, in early middle age.

The evidence of the fate in store for them is before their eyes every day in the form of their over-forty colleagues.

The fact that the sight of these stroke-prone, chesty, over-weight gentlemen in no way deters your work-mates from their unsavoury habits is yet another bit of proof that men aren't as sensible as they make themselves out to be.

The 'Don't Bother Your Pretty Head' Ploy

To make the right decisions people need information. Know-ledge is power, and to keep people in ignorance is to keep them in their place.

Sooner or later the day will come when your boss or a senior colleague will say something like, 'I don't want to inflict these figures on you, so I'll just go ahead and write this report myself if you like. I've got all the information here, and it will save the trouble of two of us going through it all twice.' Thus presenting you with a *fait accompli*. The fact that your boss is actually offering to do your job for you should certainly prompt you to question his motives.

The fact that he is no longer prepared to delegate may mean

he is worried that you are progressing too fast for his liking. He *may* be genuinely concerned that you are overworked, but you should not take it for granted.

'I've got all the information, so I'm just trying to save you aggravation by putting this analysis together, I know you've got a lot on your plate,' is a variant of this tactic, as is 'So-and-so phoned about the new contract while you were out, and as I didn't want to worry you, I just went ahead and dealt with it.'

What he hopes you'll conclude is that you're not really quite bright enough to carry out these jobs properly and that they are better left to someone more experienced, i.e. superior. He has also denied you access to some information which *might* have been useful.

It's quite all right to let him take on some of your work occasionally, it gives you more time for other things, but don't let it become a habit.

If your boss isn't just trying to cut you down to size, but actually to get rid of you, this could be his way of suggesting your job is surplus to requirements.

The 'When Are You Thinking of Retiring' Tactic

The general rule that women, unlike men, retire at sixty, gives men a trump card in the put-down stakes when they are dealing with older women.

A woman in her middle or late fifties whose boss is feeling threatened by her arrival in the upper echelons may find him starting to drop hints.

'By the way, when are you thinking of retiring?' he will ask solicitously, implying that your age and frailty are giving him cause for concern.

Despite the fact that women live longer than men, a man of sixty is regarded as being in the prime of life, so the inference that you are getting past it at that age is yet another twisted bit of Masculine Logic.

Until a man is pushing sixty-five, no one would dream of

suggesting retirement to *him*. In fact a lot of businessmen consider it an impertinence for anyone to mention retirement to them before they are at least seventy.

Being only human, these pin-pricks about age may begin to get you down.

The seeds of self-doubt are being sown.

Remind yourself firmly that these innuendoes about your rapid descent into senility are offensively illogical and not to be tolerated.

Refuse to be intimidated, you will go when you are good and ready, and if you are still doing a good job, it is most unlikely that your superiors will allow you to be bullied into leaving a day before you need to.

In fact they may well ask you to stay on, confounding your insecure enemies in the process.

The Endearment Gambit

Expressions like 'Hullo, dear', 'Did you want me, dear,' or 'Thank you, dear' all sound fairly innocent and it seems churlish at first to question what sounds merely like a cosy bit of over-familiarity.

In fact when a male business associate with whom you are only slightly acquainted, calls you 'dear', it is not all that different from calling a black man 'boy', though most men would hotly deny it.

It's a piece of cheek, like using a person's christian name without permission. The fact that men would never dream of being so over-familiar with their fellow males is a give-away.

Such expressions as 'dear', like christian names, are only normally used between close friends or relatives and the use of them in an office context is a bit of a liberty to put it mildly. Luckily you can put a full stop to it very quickly.

Next time a man you hardly know brings a file in to your office and says 'Here you are, dear,' say 'Thanks, dear.' (Or even 'duckie'.) He'll be so surprised, he'll never call you 'dear' again.

The 'Mr and Mrs' Ploy

If you are a married woman, a minor irritant in the put-down stakes can be the invitation you get to a company function. Your pleasure at being invited to what is perhaps a rather exclusive gathering of top executives and their wives may be marred by the fact that the invitation is addressed to your husband and that on the card 'the Directors have pleasure in inviting Mr and Mrs Joe Bloggs' to the festivities.

Even in these more enlightened days, society is so conditioned to the idea that a woman is her husband's chattel that even if your spouse is a drunken lay-about, dependent on you for financial support, it will still be assumed that he is the guest and you are his appendage. The only way round this is to become a DBE.

The MCP's who issue the invitations will then have no option but to describe you as 'Dame Veronica and Mr Joe Bloggs' accordingly.

The 'Territorial or Flanking' Ploy

Although most men no longer actually treat their women as property, they have still got the idea that your property is theirs.

They should be quickly disabused of this assumption.

A man who considers himself senior to you, although there may be no basis for his belief, may decide to try and pull some rank on you by invading your territory, assuming *droit de seigneur* over your furniture and fittings. To your amazement you could one day find him poking about among your cupboards or searching through the files in your cabinet.

Your instinct may be to smack him on the wrist and ask him what he is up to.

This is perfectly permissible, but it will make him look a fool in front of the secretarial staff, and a man who has been made a fool of is a dangerous enemy.

In order to avoid the tedium of an all-out battle with him, you must be more subtle.

Ask him politely what he's looking for, and get yourself some keys.

The 'Invisible Woman'

Senior staff meetings provide the background for another popular trick employed by male speakers who resent the arrival of women on the scene, feel that their presence is irrelevant, or, due to a genuine blind spot, overlook the fact that they are there at all.

The object of these regular management meetings is to raise morale and 'motivate' the assembled managers into urging their staff to greater efforts on the company's behalf.

One of the directors will get up on the platform and launch into an inspiring Henry v-at-Agincourt type of speech.

'Gentlemen,' he will begin, even though there may be a woman or two right under his nose in the front row, 'our company is going forward to greater things,' or something to that effect. He will go on to refer to the 'wives and families' of those present, and to describe what is expected of the perfect manager. 'He' will do this or that and 'his' aims will be so and so.

The speech, in short, will have been addressed to an exclusively male audience.

After one of these occasions, I was bold enough to take issue with the director concerned. Next time I was in his office on another matter, I said, 'I thought your speech at the conference was splendid, but do you realize that you were addressing it to men only?'

To my amazement, he burst out laughing.

'Now look here,' I said, pushing my luck on behalf of womankind, 'we few females have worked jolly hard to get where we are. How would you feel, being ignored by your bosses and treated publicly as though you didn't exist?'

Being at heart a kindly and reasonable man, he at once apologized. It truly hadn't occurred to him, he said, that we might feel excluded.

Some bosses are fond of referring to their executives as 'chaps'. In his address a boss will use such phrases as, 'You chaps are doing a splendid job.'

I once remonstrated politely with one of these gentlemen, pointing out that I wasn't actually a chap. 'Chaps include chapesses!' he explained, giving me a friendly pat on the shoulder.

This is all in the tradition of the famous entry in the *Encyclopaedia Britannica*, spotted many years ago by Virginia Woolf. When she looked up 'WOMAN', all it said was '*See* MAN'.

Put-Down Remarks - A Selection

'*As a woman*, what do you think of so-and-so?'

'Well, of course, I think it's really a job for a *man*.'

'Women are much better at *detailed* work don't you think.'

'You seem to be doing awfully well – *for a woman*.'

'I'm so glad you're enjoying your job, Veronica. You seem to have found yourself a nice little *niche*.'

'I shall be away tomorrow, so I'd like you to chair the weekly meeting – *if you feel you're strong enough*.'

Lack of 'strength' is often used as a reason for not giving a woman a chance at something. As this can't mean physical strength – unless the meeting is to end in fisticuffs – it must imply some kind of mental or personality defect inherent in the 'weaker' sex.

'You seem to be getting on very well with the Chairman. Of course *he's terribly weak with women*.'

'She's very clever. Of course she's got a *man's brain*.'

'I like old so-and-so but he's a bit of an *old woman*.'

You will see from the last two remarks that to describe a man as behaving like a woman is an insult, but to say that a woman thinks like a man is a compliment.

Are such seemingly trivial remarks as these really worth making a fuss about, you may ask.

Well, yes, they are.

They are the symptoms, the outward and visible signs, of the deep-rooted prejudice that runs through our society. By allowing them to pass without comment you are in a sense conniving at and reinforcing the very prejudices which are holding you back in your career.

By drawing attention to them, you are at least encouraging their perpetrators to rethink their attitudes.

Every little helps in getting the message through – that a woman in business can be every bit as good as a man, and sometimes better.

More of an irritation than a put-down is the habit that male (and I'm afraid female) executives have of assuming, when they ring your department, that because you are a female, you must be somebody's secretary.

The ultimate put-down is to be given a pat on the head.

The appropriate answer to this one can only be a karate chop.

Weeping as a Weapon

All the put-downs you have to contend with may make you wonder about the effect of crying as an anti-put-down weapon.

It Is Not Recommended

Weeping is the nuclear deterrent of the office war, only to be used when everything else has failed.

It is also strictly not cricket, though you may decide that as the males in your organization are playing such a dirty game, it is amply justified.

The main drawback is that crying is very damaging to your own morale.

The fact that you have had to resort to this ancient female trick is a reflection on your conduct of the campaign to date.

Somewhere along the line your strategy has gone badly awry.

You should be ashamed of yourself, and you probably will be.

The effect on a man of a woman crying in his office is quite sensational, causing bewilderment, embarrassment, horror, shock and the urge to run for cover.

It will almost certainly get you what you want – *but only in the short run.*

Even if you only do it *once*, it will never be forgotten. You will be branded as emotional, unstable, a typical female, unfit for a responsible, top job.

So, for all these reasons, my advice is – DON'T.

9
Passover Time

> Who loses and who wins; who's in, who's out.
>   *Shakespeare*, King Lear

Getting passed over for promotion is an occupational hazard for all executives, male and female, but as a woman you are far more at risk than a man.

If you are efficient, hardworking and next in line for promotion, and yet get passed over for that higher job, you should ask yourself as objectively as you can, 'Had I been a man, would I have been promoted?'

The answer is almost certainly yes.

An acquaintance of mine went through just such a harrowing experience.

Her case history (and her reaction) is so typical and so common to women in business that I reproduce it here, as told in her own words:

I never thought I would ever have anything in common with George Nathaniel Curzon – that 'most superior person' – the first and last Marquess Curzon of Kedleston.

He wanted to be Prime Minister. I wanted to be head of my department. Neither of us got the job. We were both passed over in mysterious circumstances.

In 1923, the Prime Minister Bonar Law resigned because of ill-health, which raised the question of his successor. Lord Curzon, confident that he was the obvious choice, retired to his estate in Somerset for the weekend to await the expected summons from King George V.

Recently the head of my department resigned to take another job. I retired to my Kensington pad for the weekend to await a call from the Boss, to tell me the good news. To my friends it was a foregone conclusion.

In due course Curzon received a telegram from the King's Private Secretary summoning him to London. He made a triumphal return, cheered by his tenants and welcomed by the press at

97

Paddington. But unknown to him, there had been dirty work afoot.

In his absence Stanley Baldwin had hatched a plot and it was Baldwin who became the new Prime Minister. When Curzon heard the news, he burst into tears.

I didn't get a phone call, but on my return to work on Monday morning, I was hailed by my colleagues as I went up in the lift. I waited in my office for a summons from the Boss. It never came. Instead, the Boss announced to the assembled department that he intended to advertise the post. I didn't burst into tears. Perhaps we live in a less emotional age.

Curzon had been Viceroy of India, Foreign Secretary and a Cabinet Minister. He considered himself ideally suited for the job of Prime Minister. A lot of other people agreed with him.

I had been with my company for ten years. I was at least as intelligent, experienced and efficient as my predecessor, for whom I had often deputized. I assumed I would get the job. So did a lot of other people.

Curzon felt he had been badly done by. He took to his bed for two days and brooded on his failure. Afterwards George v apologized to him personally, explaining that the time had come when it was no longer appropriate for a Prime Minister to sit in the House of Lords.

Nobody apologized to me, and there was no explanation. Like Curzon, I brooded. Was there a Stanley Baldwin somewhere in the firm, plotting against me? Was I too eccentric? Too old? The wrong sex? Had my husband been inspected and found wanting?

At least Curzon was told the news in private beforehand. *At least* he got some sympathy and an explanation in good faith from the King (even though it was not exactly the true one, as history has since revealed).

Funnily enough, men are usually very considerate to each other when it comes to passover time. (George v, as we have seen, apologized to Curzon.) All things being equal, a boss will usually let an executive know if he is about to be by-passed in the race for promotion.

He will do a lot of explaining and apologizing, and do his best to smooth his colleague's hurt feelings.

As a female, however senior or deserving of advancement, it is most unlikely that any such consideration will be extended to you.

A female must *expect* men to move in over her.

No explanation or apology will be considered necessary.

So, a procession of mediocre males may well pass over your head on their way to higher things – if you allow it to happen.

After the first time, you may decide to give your boss another chance.

You should certainly ask him for an explanation.

This is only fair to him. Like so many men, he may simply be suffering from short-sightedness where females are concerned.

Nowadays, you can mention the Equal Opportunities Act, though as one boss put it in a give-away remark, 'Oh, we don't want to get into all *that*!'

The natural reaction to being passed over is to hand in one's resignation at once. Except in very rare circumstances (see page 101) – DON'T.

But waste no time. Start looking for another job.

And don't announce your departure until you've got one.

The Treatment

Being passed over is part of what I call 'The Treatment'.

At some stage in your career *you* may find yourself on the receiving end of The Treatment.

It is a situation in which you suddenly, or sometimes only gradually, realize that you have been removed from the main stream of company activity. Or rather the stream has removed itself from *you*, leaving you marooned in a backwater.

It begins to dawn on you that you are seeing far less of the top executives than you used to.

People who normally consult you before taking action begin to ask other people's advice instead.

The head of your division sends for you less frequently.

The telephone doesn't seem to ring so often.

A sinister silence descends upon your formerly busy office.

There are two possible explanations.

1. It may be a geographical accident resulting from a re-organization or restructuring of the company's activities.

In this case, it will be only temporary.

2. The situation may be deliberate. Someone, or a group of people, is trying to get rid of you.

The Treatment, in my experience, is often a blessing in disguise.

Setbacks can be a good thing, forcing you out of your complacency and making you take stock.

Is it time to move?

10
Resignation Time

You can't do what you think is right without causing somebody pain or inconvenience.

Somerset Maugham, A Writer's Notebook

Having said that you should never resign unless you have another job to go to, I am now going to describe a set of circumstances in which it may be necessary for you to make the grand gesture and resign whether you have another job to go to or not.

This involves a major event with far-reaching consequences for your future – a direct confrontation and showdown with your boss, something normally to be avoided at all costs.

Laying your job on the line requires a lot of self-confidence and ice-cool nerves.

It is not recommended for the faint-hearted.

Threatening to resign is something you can only really do once, and you mustn't be shown to be bluffing. If you are, your credibility will be gone for ever.

The very fact that you are considering this major step, probably means that you are falling out of love with your job anyway and the event which has caused you to threaten resignation has merely acted as a trigger.

If you are in the fortunate position of having no financial responsibilities like children or aged relatives or even an out-of-work husband, you may actually be doing the right thing by walking out.

Having to go on in a job, however well-paid, in which you feel frustrated and unhappy, is a soul-destroying process, in which you will become broody and resentful, ending up as a sort of human vegetable.

These human vegetables are to be seen in every company,

most numerously in those from which all people of drive and initiative have long since departed.

Weighed down with mortgages, families and other commitments, too timid to stand up for themselves, these unfortunate creatures eke out a miserable existence, with only their retirement day as the light at the end of the tunnel.

You only have one life to live: why waste it, unless you really have no alternative?

Most women who suddenly find themselves out of work have an advantage over men. They have a trade to fall back on – yes, dear old shorthand and typing.

Remember, secretaries are pretty well paid these days.

You could start again at the bottom and work up.

Unless you are truly hooked on the grand life-style to which you have been accustomed, you will be better off scrubbing floors as a free spirit than continuing under the oppressive circumstances of your well-paid position as a senior executive.

Another factor to consider when you are making this dramatic move is that, surprisingly enough, it is easier for a woman to find another job when she has just left one.

Had you been a man, you would almost certainly by now have been approached by a head-hunter and offered a job with another company.

Head-hunters don't like women – for all the usual cliché reasons, marriage, babies and general 'unreliability', indeed they have gone on record as saying so.

Other people who know you and would like to employ you are frightened of being accused of poaching, something which is regarded as tantamount to an act of war among captains of industry.

Once you are a free agent, you will find yourself getting 'rescue' offers from all sorts of gentlemen who will see themselves as chivalrously coming to the aid of a maiden in distress without, in this case, running the risk of antagonizing your ex-employer.

It is usually inadvisable simply to walk out without a fight.

You might as well learn something from the experience, and the events which follow the announcement of your threatened resignation will give invaluable insights into the handling of office politics, which will come in very useful in the future.

It takes a lot more guts for a woman to resign than for a man.

A man is brought up to be aggressive and defiant. Standing up for himself and refusing to be bullied are actions secretly approved of by his superiors who will admire him for his manly and courageous behaviour.

As a woman you are flying in the face of years of conditioning and centuries of tradition.

In our paternalistic society it is accepted that a woman faces swift retribution should she impertinently fail to show proper obedience and respect to the elders of her tribe.

This awesome gallery of father figures presents a formidable list: God; the Archbishop of Canterbury; the Vicar; your Father; your Grandfather; your MP; your Doctor; your Commander-in-Chief in the war (if you are of that vintage); assorted Judges; Policemen; Uncles; Head Waiters; Lord Mayors; Schoolmasters; Industry Bosses; Shop Stewards; Union Leaders and TV Pundits.

Suddenly all these will become symbolically personified in the figures of your boss and his superiors – the tribal gods you are about to defy.

Once you have made up your mind to leave, dismiss your guilty feelings. Do not be intimidated. Hellfire and outer darkness do not await you, for these are only cardboard ogres.

In a free society, everyone has the basic right to withdraw their labour. And that includes you.

11
Showdown Time

Let us make an honourable retreat.
Shakespeare, As You Like It

So let us now consider the sort of circumstances in which you may be prepared to resign and in which you are inviting a direct confrontation with your boss.

Say, for instance, that the company you work for is doing very badly (another good reason for leaving) and your boss has been ordered by the accountants to cut his staff.

He may decide to swing the axe all round, chopping a chunk indiscriminately off each of the sections under his control.

This is a fairly common procedure in large organizations with financial problems.

You may decide that you are already stretched and that you cannot operate with fewer people in your team without seriously affecting the efficiency of your department, thereby putting your own professional reputation at risk.

Having decided that this is a matter of principle, you must always give your boss plenty of opportunity to back down.

After you have discussed the proposed cuts and made it plain that you cannot accept them, give him time to think. Whether he will be prepared to lose a valuable executive and thereby incur the irritation of his superiors is anybody's guess.

If he is sensible he will want to discuss the matter with you and try to persuade you to change your mind.

However, men are not noted for sense, as we have seen. They are quite capable of cutting off their noses to spite their faces and he may opt for treating your actions as deliberate provocation.

He may take it upon himself to lecture you on your duty to the company, which is to accept the cuts and 'soldier on' as best you can.

Duty is in the eye of the beholder and your first duty must be to yourself.

Put your views to him in writing, making it clear that you are not prepared to accept his decision, however regretfully.

'More in sorrow than in anger' is the line to take.

This letter should not be too threatening. Nobody likes being blackmailed or faced with an ultimatum. Written ultimatums should only be used in the last resort.

Make it clear that though you are serious, the door is still open and you are prepared to talk.

In the meantime, consider your next move.

This involves your boss's superiors. If you have been following the advice contained in this book, you will already be well in with all the top people in the company.

They depend on you for all sorts of extra services which you have obligingly carried out for them on a regular basis as part of your job.

They should also by now appreciate your value to the company and feel genuinely dismayed at the thought of your departure.

Nobody is indispensable, but you need to be as nearly indispensable as can be.

Next time you find yourself alone with one of these gentlemen or standing near him at a company function, drop a confidential hint that you are considering quitting the company.

Leaving no doubt as to the circumstances so that there will be no misunderstanding in the future, whether you leave or not.

This will ensure that nobody, after the event, can be left with the impression that you have been sacked.

If your eminent confidant appears suitably aghast at your news, the signs are good.

The more numerous and powerful your allies are the more creditably you will emerge from the impending conflict, whatever the final outcome. Even if you leave the company, your reputation as a woman of principle will have been preserved.

After the first shock at the news of your impending departure, your distinguished listener will demand to know what exactly is behind this turn of events.

Let him drag it out of you. Most top executives love gossip (because of their position, they hear so little of it).

To an outsider it might appear strange that directors of large companies, who normally spend their time making decisions affecting thousands of people and involving millions of pounds, should be expected to concern themselves with such petty squabbles as yours with your boss.

On the contrary, hearing about such comparatively trivial disputes provides them with a bit of welcome light relief from the burdens of office.

They have been known to treat the whole thing as a hilarious joke and fall about laughing, rather unkindly, at the thought of your boss's embarrassing predicament.

Although this war of nerves will continue to be officially carried on in secret, every clerk and secretary in the division will know that a power struggle is afoot.

They will be sitting on the sidelines placing bets on the outcome and thoroughly enjoying every move in the game.

Rumours and counter-rumours will fly in all directions.

In this situation you should remain calm and cheerful, which will make your unfortunate boss feel even more nervous and apprehensive.

Those members of your staff over whom the hatchet is suspended deserve special consideration at this time.

Take them into your confidence and explain that you are fighting tooth and nail to save their jobs.

Tell them that you trust them not to discuss what is going on with their fellow workers but that you will let them know their fate as soon as possible.

They will respect your confidence and will become your loyal friends. Should you leave the company they will probably come with you, forming a reliable nucleus of supporters in your next position.

As you have refused to sack these people, your boss will be forced to sack them himself, automatically casting himself in the role of villain, and take the consequences.

By this time your senior colleagues in the department will have got wind of what is happening.

They have already agreed to cut their staffs, and are standing by to see if you win the battle to retain yours.

They may be envious of your success and may have been plotting your downfall.

Backing down and staying on in your job just to spite them is a silly idea, and I trust you would not entertain it.

Should you triumph, these colleagues will be the first to march into your boss's office and demand the reasons for your preferential treatment, possibly even threatening to resign themselves.

Your hapless boss is now right up a creek of his own creation with no paddles in sight. Imagine his situation.

He has committed himself to sacking your underlings, but if he does, he knows that you may resign. He may go ahead with the sackings in the desperate hope that you are bluffing, but he has no way of knowing if you are or not.

If you are not, and your resignation arrives on his desk, he is risking the certain irritation of his superiors, who will blame him for losing a useful employee through what they will probably regard as simple mismanagement on his part.

Should he agree to your keeping the wretched staff who are the bone of contention, he knows your colleagues are lying in wait to tear him limb from limb and accuse him of gross favouritism.

Having by now offended just about everybody concerned, he will find himself without sympathizers in a cold and friendless world.

Your boss has probably landed himself in this predicament by making the common masculine mistake of seriously underrating your toughness, just because you are a female.

There are only three ways the dilemma can be resolved.

Either you resign, the boss resigns, or the others resign.

Your boss will now have no alternative but to go to his superiors and explain the situation.

They, unless they are prepared to break all the company rules, will have no alternative but to back him up in his decision to cut your staff.

After all, the man is only carrying out an official directive and has the law on his side. You are going to have to go.

Now is the time for you to show magnanimity. The boss needs your sympathy and understanding after his pyrrhic victory.

Show him that you are prepared to kiss and make up.

People have short memories and soon the whole episode will all become part of company history.

12
How To Leave

Since there's no help, come let us kiss and part.
Michael Drayton (1563–1631)

You have decided that you are going, so don't hang around.

If you do, you run the risk of facing an awkward farewell office party, at which biscuits and glasses of sweet sherry will be handed round by the office junior.

Your boss will make a rather nervous speech, wishing you well in your future career and presenting you with a sheaf of mauve chrysanthemums covered with transparent polythene and decorated with yellow satin bows. With this bouquet will come an enormous card almost certainly covered in pink poodles with black eyelashes.

Inside will be the signatures of everyone in the department, with suitably jokey messages from the office wags.

Over the last few weeks, the boss's secretary will have been laboriously collecting these signatures plus the contributions (£1 from the executives, 10p from the rest) towards your farewell present.

All this can be avoided if you arrange to depart discreetly on a Friday, leaving your boss to say your farewells on the Monday. Thus you will save all concerned both money and embarrassment.

An interesting by-product of the resignation syndrome is the discovery of who your best friends in the company really are. Those who rush to your support often turn out to be the last people from whom such loyalty was to be expected.

Never Go Back

There is no reason why you should not, when you are settled in your new job, invite some of your old cronies out to lunch. One meets some of one's best friends whilst working in different companies.

But don't keep going back to the building like a murderer revisiting the scene of his crime. This shows a morbid, retrospective attitude, quite unsuitable for the forward-looking dynamic executive you should have by now become.

Your bosses may be deeply pained at what some of them will see as your ungrateful and rebellious behaviour, but they will never say so.

There is no room for sentiment in business.

You may find yourself cut off like a disinherited daughter – your 'name never mentioned in the Mess' again.

All that remains for you to do now is to write a short note to all your business contacts inside and outside the company, explaining that you have resigned and are open to offers.

In the meantime brush up your shorthand and typing, you may need it.

Moral of this story – never start a war unless you are prepared to lose it.

13
'Down the Labour'

After the euphoria of your resignation, don't be tempted to loll about at home, drinking champagne and waiting for the offers to roll in.

Get down to your local Department of Employment (it's in the phone book) and SIGN ON.

There are good reasons for this.

You have been contributing a slice of your hard-earned income to the Government ever since you started work.

You are *entitled* to this money, so why not claim it?

It may seem like peanuts compared with what you have been making, but at least it may help to pay the drinks bill.

If you are lucky enough to get yourself sacked, your unemployment payments will begin from the day you left your job.

If you have resigned, the D. of E. will give you a nanny-ish slap on the wrist by denying you your money for the first six weeks.

Signing on also means that your 'stamp' will continue to be paid by the Government on your behalf.

This 'stamp' ensures that should you fall on really hard times, you will still be entitled to your unemployment money without having to fall back on National Assistance, or Supplementary Benefit, as it is now called.

Above all, a visit to the D. of E. is an enriching experience.

'All human life', as they say, 'is there.' It will also do you good to see how the other half lives.

Having listened for years to complaints about the unhelpfulness and rudeness of civil servants, you will probably be surprised by the patience and kindness of the staff.

Even the most idiotic of questions will be taken seriously and answered in detail.

For some reason, unemployed people seem to be heavy smokers and you may have to spend quite a lot of time, at least to start with, sitting beneath a pall of smoke, waiting your turn to be interviewed.

Once you have seen all the people you need to see, and filled in all the necessary forms, all you have to do is call in once a week at a specified time, and a regular cheque (known as the 'Giro') will be sent to you at home.

If you are married, you must check that you have been paying the Class One contribution, to qualify for unemployment benefit. If you have only been paying the married woman's contribution, which is much less, you may find that your husband is expected to support you while you are out of work. This could make you unpopular at home, as fewer and fewer men seem to see themselves as the sole breadwinner these days. On the contrary, an increasing number of them are beginning to enjoy the idea of actually being 'kept' – an interesting trend.

Anthropologist Margaret Mead once discovered a tribe in which this role-reversal was complete. The women made all the decisions and ran the tribe, while the men stayed at home, adorning themselves and following 'artistic' pursuits.

Maybe I struck lucky, but my own experience 'down the Labour' was a happy one.

At my local branch, Hythe House, Hammersmith, my signing-on day was Wednesday, and I soon got to know some of the staff quite well. At Christmas, a homely atmosphere prevailed, the office was adorned with festive decorations and a large notice appeared which read 'HAPPY CHRISTMAS, WEDNESDAY SIGNERS'.

The supervisor, or 'King of the Wednesday Signers', was a charming Scot called Mr Lightbody, who went out of his way to guide me through the red tape jungle.

When I congratulated him on his efficiency, he told me that considering that his particular branch had about six thousand people to cope with, he didn't think they were doing too badly. I couldn't agree more.

What to Wear 'Down the Labour'

Furs and jewellery are definitely *out*, but there is no need to go to the other extreme and try to disguise yourself as a vagrant who has been sleeping rough on the Embankment.

Something unobtrusive would be more appropriate.

14
A Few Tips for the Top

There is always room at the top.
Daniel Webster (1782–1852)

The Early Bird

The human race is divided into Larks and Owls. The Larks are up and about at the crack of dawn. The Owls don't really start to tick until late morning.

You will soon discover, during your regular chats with the receptionist or the security man, which of the directors come in early.

Mr x, you will hear, is in at 7.45 sharp every morning. Next time you have any reason to see Mr x, mention to him that you will be in to see him first thing tomorrow if that is convenient.

He will say, 'I am in at a quarter to eight,' expecting you to look horrified.

'I know,' you should calmly reply. 'I will be there.'

Set your alarm for dawn and be in the building by 7.30.

When Mr x arrives, he will find you sitting outside his office looking cool and collected.

The effort you have made will be well worth the shock to your system.

After all, you only need to do it once to make a lasting impression on this distinguished Lark.

Most of these early starters only arrive at the office at such unreasonable hours in order to upstage and impress their colleagues.

Apart from reading any telex messages which may have come in during the night, there isn't an awful lot you can do at such a time.

The post hasn't arrived and it's no good trying to do any telephoning in the UK or America as most of the English-speaking world is still in bed.

So Mr x will have plenty of time to chat to you undisturbed by visitors or phone calls.

A Lift to Higher Things

The role of lifts in corporate life has been much underrated.

Time is what most powerful men are short of, and time is what you need if you are going to impress them.

Apart from the early morning when you can get him alone, it is possible to trap a director in the lift.

Even in the few seconds involved, you can make a good impression.

Most people, finding themselves alone in a lift with a member of the top brass, will try to appear as inconspicuous as possible, staring straight ahead without speaking, except perhaps for a mumbled 'good morning'.

You are not most people.

Say 'good morning' (or 'good evening') politely and look your quarry straight in the eye.

Follow up with some flattering remark such as 'I saw your picture in the paper yesterday.'

The fact that you are a woman, that you know who he is, and that you are not afraid to address him, will start him wondering who you are. An impression will have been made.

Memos

If you want to be a top person, you should start by behaving like one.

Never write a memo when you can make a phone call.

You will soon notice that the more powerful a man is, the less paper emanates from his office.

The filling up of reams of paper with long-winded sentences

is strictly the prerogative of those small-minded bureaucrats we know so well.

So get into good habits early.

Upside Down Reading

The higher up an executive is in the hierarchy, the more important and confidential are the papers on his desk.

Unfortunately, should you happen to be in his office, you are normally on the wrong side of the desk to read them.

Cultivate the art of reading upside down. It comes quickly with practice, and you will soon find that in a few seconds you can grasp the gist of a top secret memo, while the executive concerned is momentarily distracted by a telephone call.

What to Wear at the Top

There are several ways of approaching the clothing problem for top women executives.

You can just opt out and go to Jaeger for everything. If there isn't a branch nearby, just go and stock up once every six months.

I don't want to sound like a commercial, but for elegant, dateless, trouble-free dressing for those who hate shopping or have no time, it really is the ideal solution.

Obviously the business you are in must affect your style to some extent.

One extremely successful lady TV executive used to come to work in a nightdress and nobody blinked an eyelid. Nor did this prevent her promotion to even dizzier heights.

If you are an architect visiting a building site, you can just put on a tin hat and overalls and merge with the crowd, but if you have to appear at a board meeting, you will have to give the matter some serious thought.

As a rule, looking too fashionable, in whatever style, can be distracting to your male colleagues.

Unless you are deliberately setting out to ruin their concentration for strategic reasons of your own, it's better to eschew the latest look, be it Gipsy, Ethnic, Russian Princess, Male Impersonator, or Thirties revival.

All the Trimmings

Top people's offices are usually well equipped with cocktail cabinets, hi-fi, fridges, TV sets, etc.

You will have to acquire them if you are to give the right impression to your visitors.

But first you will have to convince yourself that the level of these business visitors is such that these trimmings can really be justified.

It is advisable to avoid the usual channels when planning the acquisition of these luxuries.

Filling in forms and writing out cheque requisitions in triplicate will only draw attention to what you are up to. There are very few objects which cannot be bought perfectly legitimately with petty cash, so start modestly with a small drinks cupboard and perhaps an unobtrusive mini fridge and work up from there.

How to Read a Balance Sheet

All top people can read a balance sheet, or like to give the impression that they can.

Strangely enough, though numeracy is a help, it doesn't appear to be essential in business life.

In this connection it is worth noting that Edison, so I'm told, couldn't add up and that Nelson suffered badly from sea-sickness. Serious drawbacks, one would have thought, which in no way seem to have affected their chosen careers.

Reading a balance sheet is like making an omelette or baking a loaf of bread, an activity hedged around with folklore and mystique.

In fact it's perfectly simple when you know how.

As you move up the business ladder, one of the things you will learn is the lengths specialists go to cloak what they do with their own jargon. Nowhere is this truer than in the financial world where accountants have a language of their very own.

Don't despair however. This is a field where a little learning can stretch a long way. And whatever you do, don't ignore balance sheets and so on as a grey area of no relevance to you. Increasingly these days, big concerns are being run by ex-accountants and very often the finance director is only a stone's throw away from the top job. Moreover, in a male-orientated world that considers the only figure a woman has a head for is her own, some familiarity with balance sheets, profit and loss accounts and perhaps even more technical terms like 'gearing' or 'cash flow' is going to stand you in very good stead indeed.

The first thing to grasp is that the accountant's role is to reduce the complexities of business into a few sets of figures. Think of him as a map-maker who has to select just the right amount of detail without confusing the overall picture. An Ordnance Survey map may be fine if you're out on a country walk. It's not much help if you are trekking overland to India.

So with accountancy. Burrow deep in the finance department and you'll find the Ordnance Survey work being done – you may even come up against it if you fail to fill in your expense form correctly. But at the end of the day what top management, outsiders and you, if you are heading for higher things, are interested in is the overall picture. And that means a passing knowledge of what information is conveyed in the balance sheet and the profit and loss account.

Provided you don't get too bogged down in the details, there is nothing difficult about this. The balance sheet is a bit like an end-of-term school report. Or as accountants like to call it a financial snapshot on a particular date. The profit and loss account is simply how much money a company makes (or loses) from trading throughout the year.

The aim of the balance sheet is to show as clearly as any set of figures can the financial health of the company at the end of every year. You are well on the way to understanding the nature of balance sheets if you take a statement like that with a pinch of salt – or at least a healthy dose of scepticism. Just as you can disguise the symptoms of an illness for a while, so a good accountant can camouflage troubles within his company with some fancy financial footwork.

Essentially though the balance sheet is no more than a list of the assets of a company – machinery, land, trucks and so on – set against what it owes which is called its liabilities. Most confusion arises over why these two items always balance since in our personal finances one is invariably larger than the other. In the normal course of business there will be a number of claims on the company – bank loans, creditors and so on. And in the last resort there is always one final claimant on the assets of a business and that is the people who put up the money to start it in the first place – in the case of a big public company its shareholders.

Unfortunately, reading a balance sheet is more of an art than a science, largely because it is often very difficult to put a money value on many assets. What is a piece of machinery worth if you can't ever sell it? One favourite trick of companies to improve the look of the balance sheet is to revalue their property. More often than not, though, a company chooses to hide its light under a bushel by undervaluing its land and buildings, and this fact has been the stimulus behind many of the City takeover bids in the past.

Another item to be wary of is 'goodwill' which represents the value a company puts on itself over and above the money value of its assets. Well-known trade names like Cartier and Gucci are obviously worth a great deal should they ever come to be sold. But it is difficult to put a precise value on these and most companies these days write off their goodwill quickly.

There are a whole series of mathematical sums that can be done to assess whether a balance sheet is conservative or about to explode – such as whether the level of stocks is too high, whether the company can generate enough money to keep it ticking over (that is the cash flow item I mentioned earlier) or whether it is spending too much on new machinery or other 'fixed' assets like land or buildings. If any of these items change radically from one year to another then start asking why. Perhaps the main thing that you should keep an eye on is the level of debt in a company.

You and I can go on borrowing from our bank manager for a while but that money has to be paid back one day and in the meantime we need a higher and higher salary to go on paying the interest. It's the same with a company. Provided it can persuade its bankers it can borrow as if there were no tomorrow. But it still has to pay the interest on that money. And if interest rates go up sharply as they have done in recent years it may find it is not making enough money from trading to pay the interest. Property companies in particular have run into this problem in the 1970s. So always look in the balance sheet to see if a company's debt is increasing. If it is going up with no good reason, it is usually a danger signal. As a rule of thumb if a company's debt is much more than half the capital the owners have put in, plus the reserves it has built up over the years, which in the jargon is called a company's 'gearing', trouble could be ahead.

High finance can be a minefield. But you can take comfort from the fact that most middle managers have precious little idea of what balance sheets are about anyway and even top managers have to muddle through as best they can. Which is why I say a little learning can go a long way.

Beware of Brokers

Once you have reached the position of a senior executive in a company, you may find yourself being occasionally telephoned by stockbrokers.

A broker will ring up, introduce himself and put a seemingly innocent question to you about some of your company's operations.

Do not be deceived by these charmers.

Brokers will sometimes telephone several people in a particular company, putting the same question to each.

They will then put the answers together and get what navigators call a 'fix' on your company's financial position.

This often means that they are preparing a report for their clients on what they see as the company's prospects.

These reports, which are sometimes quoted in the financial press, can have a dramatic effect on a company's share price, sending it up or down, according to whether the report is optimistic or gloomy.

Most company bosses, though very friendly with stockbrokers, treat them with due caution, and so should you.

Financial Times Index

Anyone interested in investment, or involved in the City, will expect you to have a view about the FT Index, or to give it its full name, the Financial Times Ordinary Index.

Whenever there is an economic crisis, the state of the FT Index becomes nearly as important as the health of the pound, with radio and TV talking in gloomy tones of 'billions wiped off the value of British industry', while at City lunchtables, the FT Index is talked about almost as anxiously as a mother discussing her baby.

So what is the FT Index? It is a collection of the share prices of the thirty biggest and most representative companies in Britain. The list covers many of the best known industrial names in this country, from big drinks groups like Allied Breweries to stores like Marks & Spencer, chemical concerns like Imperial Chemical Industries and engineering ones like Lucas and Vickers. There are no banks or insurance groups since the index is meant to reflect the industrial heartland of Britain rather than its financial or commercial interests, and until British Petroleum was included a couple of years ago there were no oil groups either.

The index is carefully constructed by the *Financial Times* newspaper, to take account of the differing sizes of the various companies and broadly speaking the intention is that it should be a barometer of how investors view the prospects for British industry.

It does not always work out like this, since however important the thirty companies making up the index are, they cover only a small proportion of the concerns operating in Britain. To overcome this drawback, many prefer to work on the Financial Times All Share Index which covers 500 companies. In recent years the FT Index has also been subject to extremely wide fluctuations, which have borne little resemblance to the true outlook for the British economy. For all that, however, the FT Index has proved its mettle in the past as a good predictor of how the British economy will behave and, in City circles, it is usually thought of as working a year ahead of developments in the economy at large.

Now that you know what the FT Index is all about, the only other thing you should pay attention to is whether it is going up (a bull market in the jargon of the City) or going down (a bear market). Don't worry if people ask you if you think the index will go up or down. Past experience has shown that the amateur's guess is every bit as good as the professional's – and often a lot better.

15
Aren't You Glad You're Female?

Teach thy necessity to reason thus;
There is no virtue like necessity.
Shakespeare, Richard II

Beating the Armada

As we have seen, your disadvantages as a woman in business are immense in this hierarchical male society.

Your natural frustration at not being automatically accepted as one of the boys is something you will have to come to terms with.

But there are compensations in being a woman and they should not be underestimated.

Above all, you have the advantage of being an unknown quantity. The element of surprise is on your side.

The Spanish Armada, as every schoolgirl knows, was beaten by small, fast British ships which easily outmanoeuvred the lumbering galleons of the Spanish fleet.

Men who are unused to finding a female in their midst, attending their meetings and dealing with them on equal terms, will feel uneasy. To them, you are a person out of context so your presence is, at least to start with, *disconcerting*.

You have got the initiative, they are on the defensive and you, like the fast, small British ships, have the chance to run rings around these slow-moving, conservatively minded executives.

Assert yourself quickly before they have time to recover from the shock of your arrival and start thinking about how to put you back in your place.

In other words, they can be vanquished before they even realize that war has been declared.

The Flower Ploy

Most men are used to sitting in pretty stark offices.

They may have a few books on a shelf, some photographs of the wife and kids, an easy chair or two, but nothing much else to make themselves feel at home.

In fact most men go to the office to *escape* from home.

You as a woman can bring a 'home' atmosphere to the office and turn it to your advantage.

As well as easy chairs, you should make a point of always having fresh flowers on your desk.

These flowers are an outward and visible sign of your 'femininity' and thus a trump card in your plan to disconcert your enemies.

Nothing makes a man more nervous than having to talk business with a female across a desk decorated with highly scented red roses.

Behind this floral barrier, the poor man will feel completely at your mercy.

The Picture Ploy

According to Michael Korda in his book *Success*, men keep photographs of their families in the office to impress their superiors with their stability as family men.

As a woman, your stability will always be in question, whatever you do, so you might as well put up whatever pictures take your fancy.

Photographs of your favourite pop stars are probably unsuitable, giving an unfortunate impression of frivolity, but pictures of your pets are quite permissible. If you have a cat, by all means display its picture on your walls.

The combination of women and cats has always struck fear

into the hearts of men. Witches and their cats were frequently burnt alive in the Middle Ages, because they were suspected of being in league with the Devil and wielding secret powers.

A large portrait of your favourite Siamese, preferably wearing a suitably enigmatic expression, will help to create a pleasantly sinister atmosphere.

Refuge in the Loo

Men find it difficult to escape from their bosses.

Even in the loo they are likely to bump into them.

You have no such problems. The ladies' is your refuge where no male would dare to tread.

Whether you need a quiet ten minutes to do your nails or apply your make-up, or whether you need to shed a few tears of frustration at the way things are going, you can retire behind the loo door safe from the prying eyes of your superiors.

Catching the Boss's Eye

As we have already seen, gettting spotted by the top people in your company is important.

Should you be lucky enough to catch the eye of the chief executive, it will almost certainly be for the 'wrong' reason, i.e. your 'femininity'.

Your colleagues would regard this as an unfair advantage.

Ponder, however, on the advantages they have over you and remind yourself that there is no such thing as 'fairness' in the business world.

As I shall show later, becoming the managing director's girl friend is not recommended, but giving the impression that you *might* be, is quite another story. If you suspect that people may be jumping to conclusions, create an air of mystery. Never discuss the matter with anyone and never say anything that might be considered compromising.

It's what you *don't* say that will do the trick.

Giving the impression that you have secret power behind the throne can do no harm. In fact you may find yourself being treated by some of your more obsequious colleagues with a deference which may amuse you.

16
Keeping Sex out of It

> Business first, pleasure afterwards.
> *William Thackeray (1811–63)*

The 'Love' Interest

In films or plays an actress is often referred to as 'supplying the love interest'.

It is a fair analogy to point out that when you arrive at an all-male business meeting, you, in the eyes of your colleagues, are supplying the sex interest.

Their first reaction will be to sum up your bedworthiness or otherwise.

How attractive are you? How old are you? Are you wearing a wedding ring? If not, have you got a lover? Are you a lesbian? All this will be going through their heads before they can get down to business.

According to some observers of the office scene, men are so obsessed with sex that it's amazing they ever manage to concentrate on their jobs at all.

Certainly their reaction to a woman in their midst shows how easily they can be distracted.

This is why so many all-male institutions fight to the last ditch to keep women out, on the grounds that they are too 'distracting'.

It never seems to occur to them how distracting men can be to women.

There is nothing more irritating to a serious female who is trying to concentrate on the matter in hand at a meeting, than the realization that her attention is wandering. She has just noticed that the bloke opposite has the most amazingly long eyelashes.

Admittedly the fact that businessmen are not chosen for their eyelashes, or any other physical attributes, is a big help.

Vast numbers of them are over-weight, and their way of life is certainly not conducive to the retention of whatever looks they may once have had.

All of which of course makes the attractive ones even more noticeable.

Business and Pleasure

Should you consider taking your interest in the owner of the eyelashes any further, consider the implications.

You will be embarking on an affair with a business colleague, and business and pleasure very rarely mix.

(If you suddenly decide that the pleasure is more important than the business, well, pack in the business and go after the pleasure and the best of luck. Giving up all for love is a basic human right.)

Your boy friend, if he is so attractive to you, is also attractive to other women and therefore almost certainly married.

If he is successful in his job, he will almost certainly be wrapped up in his work, leaving little time for you.

I have seen far too many cases of unfortunate females languishing by telephones while their paramours jet from country to country and meeting to meeting, with minimum time to spare for murmuring sweet nothings down the line.

It is a most miserable state of affairs and one can only advise against getting involved in it.

You'll Be the One to Go

There is another serious snag in having an affair with someone in your company.

If too many people find out about it, and it's a difficult thing to hide, the situation may become embarrassing.

Your boy friend will almost certainly be considered more important than you are, and you are the one who will be expected to leave.

I remember a famous case in which a man and a woman, both working for the same company, started a relationship. All went well, until the girl tried to end the affair, upon which her boy friend went berserk and assaulted her with a carving knife.

After he came out of prison, the company gave him back his job. She, although the 'innocent' party, got the sack.

This is of course an extreme example, but it illustrates my point.

All in all, then, think carefully what you are doing.

The worst thing that you can do is fall in love with your boss. If that happens, for heaven's sake – GET OUT QUICK!

You won't regret it.

How to Refuse a Pass

This can be tricky, as all men are convinced that they are irresistible, and that all women who don't fancy them are 'frigid'.

The safest thing to do is to pretend you haven't noticed.

Laughing will cause resentment and almost any other reaction is fraught with danger. You are going to have to work with this man so it's essential not to ruffle his feelings unduly.

The fact that you are married or engaged will not necessarily deter your suitor. In fact some men consider that this makes you even more of a challenge.

The safest thing to do is not give the situation a chance to develop. Be pleasant to him, but make sure he never manages to get you alone, or if he does, plead an urgent engagement before he has time to open negotiations.

Spotting these potential Casanovas in advance is half the battle.

17
Are We Fair to Men?

Nobody is on my side, nobody takes part with me: I am cruelly used, nobody feels for my poor nerves.

Jane Austen, Pride and Prejudice

Don't Weaken

Some of my more squeamish readers may at this stage begin to feel that this book is getting quite unfairly anti-male. Don't weaken. Remember these tactics you have adopted are not of your own choosing. They have been forced on you by the defenders of that exclusive male bastion you are trying to storm.

Nevertheless you may still find yourself pausing to wonder whether your behaviour towards these unsuspecting males is almost too unscrupulous.

Is it really right to take unfair advantage of these innocent creatures?

Well, ask yourself honestly, would you have got as far as you have if you had left it all to them?

Would any of them lose a moment's sleep over the thought that you might have spent your whole life stuck behind a type-writer?

Would any of them have lifted a finger to get you out of that situation?

If you are honest, the answer is, no.

You've got where you are by your *own* efforts and by playing the game by *their* rules. If you have had to take to the maquis on occasion, well, that is only because you were forced to by the System.

Many men have done the same.

You have only taken the devious route when the straight course was unfairly blocked to you.

Do Men Deserve Our Sympathy?

Like most women, I was brought up to believe in the superiority of the male.

So strong was this early conditioning, that even now, with so much evidence to the contrary, I still find myself looking out for one of these legendary creatures, a superior male.

I am a born optimist and I still believe that somewhere these paragons really do exist.

In the meantime we must all accept the fact that most of the men we deal with are unlikely to come into that category, and we had just better make the best of it.

I like to believe that men are not inherently nasty.

I think they may well be basically nice people who have been 'got at' at an early age and brought up to assume that the other half of the human race is inferior and should be kept firmly in its place.

The fact that this belief is actually beginning to be questioned by men themselves is greatly to their credit.

But this early conditioning is so effective that men still feel threatened by the arrival of an ambitious woman 'out of context' in their midst.

Is it Cricket?

'First rate people hire first rate people. Second rate people hire third rate people' (quoted in Robert Townsend's *Up the Organization*).

A first rate executive hires first rate people because he prefers an efficient staff. He is so confident in his own ability that he doesn't feel threatened by them.

A second rate man, because he is insecure, is careful to hire people even less intelligent than himself. He feels safer that way.

By the law of averages, your boss is likely to be a second rater. He has either inherited you, or hired you in the belief that as a woman, you are by definition third rate, and therefore no threat.

Imagine his discomfiture when he discovers that he has a first rate female on his hands.

A man who feels threatened by a female tends to react badly.

You have, so to speak, put yourself 'beyond the pale' by your 'unfeminine', that is to say, non-submissive behaviour and you must take the consequences.

The rules of cricket, he will conclude, can be safely disregarded.

Thus a man who is normally loyal and truthful with his male colleagues will not hesitate to mislead you or even lie to you if he sees you as a threat to himself or the established, male-dominated *status quo* of his department.

Taking all these facts into account, it is unfortunately *necessary* to mistrust men and treat them with extreme caution at all times.

Feeling sorry for a man is a luxury no woman can really afford.

Men, Oh Pause!

Needless to say, there are times when men will go all out to try and get your sympathy.

It is now established that men do have some kind of menopausal symptoms, though the study of these is still in its infancy.

Unfortunately, they don't pause to think what their unhealthy life-styles are doing to them, and go along pursuing all their bad habits of smoking, downing beer and shepherd's pie at the pub, driving to and from the office and then complaining that they are suffering from *stress*.

You as a woman, they will infer, are adding to the terribly stressful situation they find themselves in. Surely you must feel some sympathy for them in their pitiable plight?

This overdramatization, heightened by the sufferer's frequent swallowing of handfuls of pills in your presence, can be quite unnerving to the uninitiated.

Keep your head and try to look tactfully away. Unless you happen to have a stiff drink handy.

This will sometimes help to relieve the stress and give the sufferer a chance to recover his equanimity.

'Nobody Appreciates Me'

Another ploy to try and get your sympathy is the 'nobody appreciates me' line.

This can be even more heart-rending than the 'stress' syndrome.

It involves haggard looks, deep sighs, late working on seemingly endless piles of paper, plus of course the usual pill-taking.

If the victim starts to refuse alcohol and takes to keeping a tray of pills and mineral water on his desk, you are faced with a serious case of the 'nobody appreciates me' blues.

This type of sympathy bid is usually adopted by the middle-aged, middle-management type of executive who is stuck in a dead-end job and who is feeling unloved and 'used' by his superiors.

Unfortunately the sorrier they feel for themselves, the more they wallow in ostentatious self-pity, the less sympathy these masochists are likely to receive from their bosses, who will continue to bully and make fun of them.

The best thing you can do is to try and help the sufferer to regain his sense of proportion and even his sense of humour. After all, having to work with someone who is in an advanced state of self-martyrdom is no fun for anybody, and the sooner you can talk him out of it the better.

18
When the Company Starts To Take Over Your Life - Watch Out!

Put not your trust in princes.
Psalms 146:2

The Shareholders Must Come First

Some people, after they have been working for a company for some time, begin to feel that they are part of a family, that the company somehow belongs to them and that they know what's best for it. Once you start identifying yourself with an organization, you are heading for dangerous ground.

The first sign that you are getting too involved is when you catch yourself referring to the company as 'we'.

Many companies deliberately encourage this kind of 'family' spirit, creating an atmosphere of cosy paternalism.

Some years ago, when I was discussing my company pension with a personnel manager, and the amount of money I would be required to contribute should I join the scheme, I expressed the opinion that my husband might be prepared to look after me in my old age.

'Nonsense!' replied this gentleman, 'you're much better off with the Corporation.'

Never forget that a company, however concerned it may appear for your welfare, is run as a business. Its first loyalty is to the shareholders to whom it owes its existence, and its main aim must be to make profits for them.

Some companies are of course privately owned, and exist to make money for the proprietors.

Either way, these companies are not in business to look after *you*.

You as a worker are simply there as a necessity. If the com-

F

pany could employ a computer to do your job, you can be pretty sure that it would do so.

With the advent of silicon chip microprocessors, that is exactly what it will do to large numbers of people.

So this sentimental approach to your employers is entirely inappropriate, however charming and fatherly they may seem.

The country is littered with bitter old men and women, some of them faithful old retired secretaries who just never knew what hit them when their beloved company, to which they had devoted so many years of their lives, began to change and become to them more and more hostile and unrecognizable.

There may have been a takeover by another company. This can be a very traumatic experience for those who have been taken over.

Those who try to fight the new regime and the new management, insisting on doing things 'the way they've always been done', are the most at risk, and will almost certainly find themselves out in the cold.

It may simply be that a new managing director has arrived with a lot of new ideas about 'modernizing' the organization.

Sooner or later, something like this will happen to the company you work for. If it doesn't, there is something wrong.

A company is a living, growing thing, continually renewing itself to suit changing circumstances and new markets.

A company which stands still will not survive.

It's up to you to change with it. Older employees are the ones who find it most difficult to adapt. To them it appears that something has gone terribly wrong with the 'family'. It is heading for disaster under this new regime, and it's up to the loyal old members of the staff to get together and save it from disaster.

They simply cannot accept that things are not what they were and probably never will be again.

They are horrified to find that their criticism of the new systems which are being introduced and their warnings of the terrible catastrophes ahead are falling on deaf ears.

Usually these people are near retirement age and very often

the company will persuade them to leave early in order to get them out of the way.

Their departure will be cushioned with all sorts of consolation prizes, like nice farewell parties with lots of reminiscences about the 'Good Old Days', polite speeches by the new management and probably a set of gardening tools or a pair of decanters.

It can all be very painful.

In nature, those species which cannot adapt to new conditions are the ones which don't survive.

The best antidote against 'company-itis' is probably to have a wide range of interests outside the office.

If you feel you haven't got time for them, and prefer to spend your life concentrating on your career, at least keep your sense of proportion by treating the whole business as an intellectual exercise, a sort of chess game with human pawns.

That, after all, is what it really is.

19
Pigeon-hole Time

> O let us love our occupations . . .
> And always know our proper stations.
> *Charles Dickens (1812–70)*

One of the occupational hazards of becoming a senior manager of the feminine gender is the risk of getting type-cast in some totally irrelevant role by your male colleagues.

Men have always had problems in accepting females as bona fide human beings like themselves and for thousands of years they have been categorizing and pigeon-holing them as Earth Mothers, Damsels in Distress, Whores, Virgins, Madonnas, Housewives, Goddesses, Witches, Bitches or whatever.

Finding you in their midst, they will immediately start casting about for a convenient pigeon-hole to put you in.

The Court Jester

One of your main problems as a woman in business will have been to get yourself taken seriously. If you happen to be of a cheerful and light-hearted disposition (and you will certainly have needed a sense of humour to get where you are) you will fit nicely into the role of Court Jester, a purveyor of light relief to the men who bear the heavy burdens of decision-making.

All the time and energy you have spent getting yourself accepted and respected will be set at naught if you allow this to happen.

By all means avoid the pomposity of your male counterparts, but on no account allow yourself to degenerate into a sort of John Brown to the chairman's Queen Victoria.

The Hostess/Social Secretary

A lot of men in top management fancy the idea of having a kind of surrogate wife in the office to organize their parties and act as unofficial hostess at board room lunches.

If you are reasonably presentable and know how to pour a Campari-and-soda, you may well find yourself falling, or being pushed, into this role, issuing invitations on behalf of your managing director, ordering the food, deciding the table plan and greeting the guests and entertaining them with light chat when the MD is held up in his office on an urgent call.

There is no harm in all this as long as you make it clear that being a hostess on such occasions is purely a side-line, and that although you may be a civilizing influence on the board room scene, this is co-incidental to your real job as an executive of the company.

The Power Behind the Throne

'A Favourite has no Friend!' (Thomas Gray).

Any woman who gets near the top of an organization and has access to the man who is the head of it, will sooner or later start to hear mutterings of 'Petticoat Government'.

Unpopular decisions by the chief executive are often laid at the door of some female who is suspected of ensnaring him with feminine wiles and cajoling or bullying him into favouring some executives or getting rid of others.

From Lady Macbeth to Lady Falkender, the Bossy Woman in the Background has always been a favourite cliché figure, often exaggerated, or even invented, by scaremongering members of the media.

These 'ogresses' are unfairly given a bad name and accused of interfering maliciously in affairs of state.

Your boss may well pay extra attention to your opinions because he respects your intelligence, but don't expect everyone else automatically to accept the fact.

If you *are* Teacher's Pet, you may well be tempted to settle a few old scores. You wouldn't be human if you didn't relish the chance to damn with faint praise some Super-Pocket who has caused you problems in the past. Try to be magnanimous. This is no time for petty revenge. If your opinion on such a man is asked, the worst you should do is refer to him as a good 'Nuts and Bolts' man.

This will put him firmly in his place as a member of the second eleven, a plodding mediocrity with no potential for the top.

20
Segregation and
Female 'Magic'

Destructive, damnable, deceitful woman!
Thomas Otway (1652–85)
How now, you secret, black and midnight hags!
Shakespeare, Macbeth

Males in primitive societies are in the habit of locking up females at certain times and seasons and isolating them from the rest of the community.

This is because they believe that women have some secret power, something to do with menstruation it now appears, which can somehow affect the crops, the harvest, or even men themselves, damaging their virility.

Sometimes the adult males hold secret initiation ceremonies in which boys are introduced to manhood.

It is taboo for women to witness these ceremonies, sometimes on pain of death. I am not just being fanciful when I suggest that men in our own society still seem to suffer from a superstitious fear that this powerful female magic could, if unleashed, adversely affect the company's operations.

Men therefore feel safer if the women in the organization are segregated into specifically defined areas of activity, i.e. secretaries, packers, assemblers of small parts, etc.

Walk round any factory and you will almost certainly observe that these areas of 'male' and 'female' production do exist.

The fact that most of the 'female' jobs pay less money is no coincidence.

The object is to limit the power of women, and money means power.

Men invent all sorts of ingenious excuses for excluding women from 'male' areas of activity.

The legal profession has produced a nicely bizarre example

145

of this kind of thinking. A lawyer friend of mine tells me that she remembers a proposal put forward quite seriously by her male colleagues that women should be banned from becoming barristers. The reason being that, as women had higher voices than men, they would be inaudible to the judge in court.

One old favourite is that separate lavatories have to be provided for women, and that there isn't enough space, or the cost would be too high.

This was apparently used for years as one good reason to keep women out of the House of Lords, and it's still being used to keep them out of the Fire Service.

Clare Dover, now Science Correspondent of the London *Daily Express*, once ran into this loo problem with an oil rig which she had been invited to visit. When the oil company discovered that 'C. Dover' was a woman, they cancelled the invitation on the ground that there was no ladies' loo aboard the rig. When it became known that other oil companies were happy to accommodate female journalists on their rigs, the ban was lifted.

Keeping the 'Balance'

This segregation of females into specific categories gives men a splendid chance to indulge in a bit of Masculine Logic.

I once worked in a department which consisted of the boss (male) and four executives (three male plus myself) and eight secretaries and clerks (all female).

When one of the male executives left, I suggested we might look for a female replacement.

My boss replied that he thought this might make the department appear 'unbalanced'. People would accuse him of employing too many females. (I have yet to hear of anyone who is accused of employing too many men.)

Obviously the department did consist of more women than men.

But the fact that the men were all at the top (executives) and the women were all at the bottom (secretaries) did not suggest any lack of 'balance' to him.

Men Are Advisers, Women are Advised

The whole business world is bedevilled by not very bright gentlemen who think they know it all.

They don't like taking advice from anyone and certainly not from a woman.

They, on the other hand, will give you plenty of advice, whether you ask for it or not, and they will expect you to take it.

Men give advice, and women follow it if they know what's good for them, that's the way they look at it.

Don't be surprised, therefore, if some new boy arrives on the scene and declines your advice on some matter in which you are knowledgeable and experienced.

Believe it or not, he would rather do it his own way and make a hash of it.

This reluctance of men to seek information from experts is well known to students of Masculine Logic.

It is a common occurrence, for instance, for a man trying to find his way while driving through a strange city, to refuse to ask anyone the way.

He'd rather get lost.

This can be most infuriating to his passengers, but there's nothing much they can do about it.

There's not much you can do about your new colleague in the office either.

Let him go ahead with his catastrophic project and steer well clear.

It may even be advisable to go on holiday until the worst is over.

21
You Mean You Really Want To Go On?

There are two things to aim at in life: first to get what you want; and, after that, to enjoy it. Only the wisest of mankind achieve the second.

Logan Pearsall Smith (1865–1946)

Nothing is so good as it seems beforehand.
George Eliot (1819–80)

Having reached the lofty heights of a senior executive, you are now in a position to enjoy the fruits of your labours.

Life at the top of a large company can become almost insidiously smooth and enervating.

Cushioned and cocooned from morning till night by a bevy of transport managers, travel departments, booking clerks, accountants and personnel officers, you live in a gilded cage.

Not for you the vulgar pressures of the rush hour, no queueing for buses or fighting for a seat on a commuter train.

Your company car, or your specially ordered limousine, will bear you smoothly to your destination.

No worries about parking need concern you. A space in the company car park will be yours, probably with your name and rank printed on the wall beside it.

Are you travelling further afield?

Your train or plane tickets will arrive gift-wrapped on your desk.

Chauffeur-driven cars will convey you to the station or the airport and will meet you on your return.

For you, the drudgery of the cold, workaday world is over.

No slaving in dingy basements, no queueing at the self-service canteen.

Your office will be an elegant retreat, your table will be booked and waiting at the restaurant of your choice. Your credit card, probably supplied by the company, or your signature, will take care of the bill.

149

The accounts department will ensure that your tax is paid and the personnel department that your health is watched over by expensive medical insurance schemes and your pension rights safeguarded for the future.

Do you want to build an extension to your house? It is unlikely that you will need to grovel to your bank manager. The company will advance you an interest-free loan.

Should you require tickets for the opera or the theatre, all you have to do is ask your secretary.

Somewhere in the building, you may be sure, there will exist an official whose job it is to ensure that the best seats in the house are yours.

If you decide to see a play which is so successful that seats for it are unobtainable, one of your top level contacts will see to it that things are arranged.

No exclusive company function, or gala premiere will be complete without you.

At such affairs you can, if you feel so inclined, hob-nob with politicians, showbiz celebrities and royalty.

To some people, such an existence seems unquestionably ideal.

They revel in it and would ask for no other. It is surprising how star-struck some otherwise level-headed businessmen can be.

It is not surprising that people who leave the company for whatever reason, and decide to go it alone, often feel like those widowed ladies whose husbands have always insisted on handling all their affairs for them – completely lost when faced with the intricacies of car insurance, income tax or pension schemes.

It can be a salutary experience.

From your vantage point near the top of the organization, you are now in a position to assess your chances of reaching the pinnacle of the company, i.e. the main board.

By now you will probably know most of the directors personally and possibly even be on christian name terms with them.

If you stand on tiptoe, so to speak, you can now peer in at the window of that holy of holies, the board room, and get a pretty good idea of what goes on there.

Most board meetings, by all accounts, are pretty routine, even tedious, affairs, and bear little relation to the dramatic picture presented in films and on TV.

Their main function is to give men the chance to indulge in the ritual and ceremony which they so enjoy, at the same time allowing them to confront each other in tests of strength.

The start of that ritualistic event, the board meeting, is heralded by the arrival outside the company's headquarters of a fleet of limousines, each with an immaculate chauffeur at the wheel.

Inside recline the deities attending the ceremony, some from abroad, some from other offices or factories of the company, some part-time consultants who spend their lives travelling from one company's board meeting to another's.

As they enter the building, bearing monogrammed leather or crocodile briefcases, and moving with appropriate gravity, the commissionaire will obsequiously open the door for each one, and the secret buttons under the receptionist's desk which control the lifts will be working overtime.

There must be no delays, no vulgar collisions with the tea-lady's trolley, as the high priests move upwards to the place of solemn conclave.

When all are present, the doors will be closed discreetly by the Chief Acolyte (the company secretary) and a hush will descend on the upper floors of the building. Even the more boisterous members of the staff seem to walk on tiptoe should their business take them within earshot of the temple doors.

The quasi-religious trappings of these all-male ceremonies cannot disguise the fact that board meetings are not only boring ('bored' meetings?), they can be a bit of a con.

The impression is that weighty affairs of state are under discussion, and that these discussions will result in epoch-making decisions with far-reaching effects.

In fact practically every decision will already have been made by the one or two really bright directors present, and the rest are simply there to 'rubber stamp' it.

This won't prevent these 'spectators' from holding up the proceedings with trivial queries, so that things may drag on almost past lunch-time, with some of the older directors drop-ping off in their chairs.

The real object of a board meeting, or any other business meeting for that matter, is not actually decision-making at all.

It is a battle-ground or tournament where a man can test his strength against his peers.

It gives these knights of commerce a chance to gather at the Round Table (oval is more common these days) and tilt at each other, as in Days of Old.

While the majority of the directors keep a low profile, or take a quick nap, the star jousters will join lances, battling it out until the chairman calls time.

Contestants and all will then repair to a suitably exclusive venue, there to refresh themselves with the choicest food and wine, and conduct a nice, chatty *post mortem* on the highlights of the tournament.

At this point in your career you may start to wonder whether you seriously want to become an active participant in these high-level rigmaroles.

Can you honestly tell yourself that these goings-on represent a meaningful way of life?

It is not surprising, and it's not just sour grapes, that at this stage in their careers some women, being extremely realistic, and having so to speak seen the Emperors without their Clothes, may begin to feel disillusioned about their role as aiders and abettors of the Corporate Life-Style.

They may decide that enough is enough, and just pack it all in.

They may opt to get married, or have a baby, or live off the land in some remote area, or go on a round-the-world trip, in an attempt to get back to some sort of reality.

This defection will inevitably be interpreted by their male colleagues as a piece of typically irresponsible female behaviour.

'That is the trouble with promoting females to top jobs,' they will say. 'You just can't rely on them to stay with the company. Off they go, to get married or whatever,' thus per-petuating the old tradition that women and business don't mix.

It is my belief that women and business *would* mix if only

men would become more businesslike, but there seems little sign of that at the moment.

If only enough women were prepared to stick with their jobs and persevere, I believe that they would, eventually, introduce a more rational approach to the way in which businesses are conducted.

There's only one snag. Men, as we have seen, *like* things the way they are. For thousands of years they have been running the world, and their businesses, to suit themselves, and they don't really *want* a lot of women arriving on the scene and insisting on introducing boring things like practical common sense and efficiency.

Because it would spoil the *fun*. Because *fun* is what men are having at the moment, doing things in their own, inimitable way.

And that, I'm afraid, is what sex discrimination in business is really all about.

22
Some Statistics To Make You Blink

Having said all this, what actually are your chances of becoming a director of the company?

Very slim indeed, I'm afraid. As far as it was possible to discover, in 1976/77, out of the top 100 British companies, only three, Woolworth's, Tesco and Tube Investments, had a woman executive director on the main board. Not surprisingly, two of them were personnel directors.

A survey on the number of women in top jobs conducted at this time revealed some interesting facts.

I doubt if things have altered very much since.

Private Industry

Rothman's had one woman president of an associated company, and nine others out of the 100 had women executive directors on the boards of subsidiaries – Thorn Electric, Grand Metropolitan, Unigate, Boots, Guinness Peat, Rank, Inchcape, EMI and Booker McConnell.

Getting information from private industry proved the most difficult for my researcher.

Twenty-four out of the 100 companies refused the information or simply did not send a reply, from which one can only assume that they have not got much to boast about in the way of female executives.

From those companies who were willing to supply information, it emerged that most female executives, where they exist at all, are almost exclusively in personnel, finance, law, public relations and buying, though Guinness came up with a chief chemist, presumably to check the ingredients of the famous stout.

Some spokesmen seemed startled at being asked about the position of women in their organizations.

One gentleman from a large catering concern which must be nameless, fell about laughing and expressed the opinion that 'women can't stay up all night selling gin to Arabs', while a lady from Esso rather let the side down by saying she wouldn't want to work for a woman.

A representative of the House of Frazer in a charming letter, gave the rather quaint reply that 'the structure of the company is so complex that it prevents analysis within the laid down criteria'.

The best Rank-Hovis could produce was 'a wages clerk', while Beechams opted out by saying that 'bald statistics lend themselves to misrepresentation'.

Lucas Industries declined politely to be drawn, on the grounds that 'we regard information of this type to be personal and confidential'.

Vauxhall Motors got straight to the point by saying with refreshing honesty that 'this company has no women in top jobs'.

Banks

The Big Four were very forthcoming.

Though their highest ranking women proved to be 'a London Recruiting Officer' (Lloyds), 'a staff manager' (Barclays), assistant staff manager (Midland) and a divisional personnel manager (NatWest), all four employed a comparatively large number of female executives in the usual fields of finance, law, personnel and public relations.

Though none of them had a woman on the board, the Midland said that 'the matter was under consideration'.

Nationalized Industries

Quite a different pattern emerged in the nationalized industries, which seem to go in for part-time non-executive women directors, particularly the Electricity Board which boasts no fewer than ten on its area boards.

British Airports Authority, British Airways, the Commonwealth Development Corporation, North and South of Scotland Hydro-Electricity Boards and the White Fish Board (what are black fish, one wonders) have one of these part-timers each.

The Coal Board took the trouble to write a most informative and lengthy letter, explaining that because women were not allowed to work down the mine, top jobs were virtually closed to them, as a period down the pit was considered a requisite qualification for a post in management.

However, in the professional fields like medical, legal and financial they are comparatively well represented.

Eastern Electricity Board were delighted to be able to send us a press release about their Mrs Georgie Moses, who had just been appointed to the post of District Administrative Officer in Peterborough, 'the first woman to reach such a senior position with any Electricity Board in Britain'.

The Atomic Energy Authority (highest graded woman the Chief Press Officer) wanted to know, 'How can scientific women be graded?'

The Civil Aviation Authority seemed unable to come up with any definite information except that they had ten men on their board and not a woman in sight.

Cable and Wireless, on the other hand, were able to tell us that they had a female group chief accountant plus 'one or two middle management managers'.

The Electricity Council's senior female executive was a senior industrial adviser, and the Central Electricity Generating Board had two managers, one deputy manager of services, and an admin. officer.

The North of Scotland Hydro-Electric Board, apart from their part-time non-executive director, had no 'senior' women members of the staff, though a large number of women performed 'invaluable roles as secretaries, senior sales staff and energy marketing officers'.

They also had a solicitor, two senior programmers and a lady in charge of 'secretarial services'.

Compared with the woman-conscious world of electricity, the Gas Corporation Board presented a dour prospect.

No women on any boards, not even part-timers.

All top positions, they told us unequivocally, were held by men.

'How many gas engineers were there, twenty years ago?' demanded a spokesman, gloomily.

Outsiders, he explained, were not encouraged. Staff were 'expected to work their way up'.

It was with relief, therefore, that we turned our attention to the Herring Industry Board of Sea Fisheries House, Edinburgh, who informed us that although their board does not number a woman among its members, 'Mrs M. E. Toynbee is the highest ranking woman among the Board's staff, and her educational background and lengthy administration experience would most certainly qualify her for inclusion in any list of Scotswomen of executive calibre.'

The Civil Service

The Civil Service Year Book is a mine of information, telling one almost 'more than one wants to know' about women in government employment.

Nevertheless, there are some startling variations which immediately strike the keen researcher.

The Department of Education and Science top the league of government departments, with a total of ninety-seven women executives in its ranks, the Home Office was next with sixty-seven and the Department of Health and Social Security with fifty-eight.

This compares with none at all in sixteen other departments (see table).

All kinds of riveting information is supplied, such as the fact that apart from Ladies-in-Waiting, the Royal Household is singularly short of female courtiers.

Ninety-two per cent of the typing in the civil service is done by women, which comes as no surprise, while 15 per cent of the legal work is carried out by female executives, which is comparatively high.

Perhaps the most interesting statistic is that in the specialist grades: women make up 31 per cent of the Scientist Officers, and 17 per cent of the Higher Scientist Officers.

The highest category to feature women is Under Secretary, Administration Open Structure, a splendidly civil service title, in which women make up 3 per cent.

Nothing much to write home about, but things do start to improve slightly further down the line, with women Higher Executive Officers (Grade A) making up 8 per cent.

Certainly the civil service seems to offer a wide range of activities, and I understand that they pay pretty well too.

Civil Service 1975/76

700,000 in the Civil Service i.e. 65%
250,000 are women   35%
Of these women 90% are non-industrial Civil Service
          10% are industrial
In the principal grades of the non-industrial
    8% are Executive Officers
   83.3% are Clerical, typing, machine operators, etc.

Table H

Group, Class or Grade	Percentage who are women
Administration, Open Structure Under Sec.	3.4
Asst. Sec.	4.8
Senior Principal	3.0
Senior Executive (SE)	7.7
Higher Executive Officer (A) (HEO (A))	8.2
Higher Executive Officer (HEO)	27.7
Administration Trainee	14.4
Executive Officer (EO)	31.3
Clerical Officer	31.7
Clerical Assistant	61.0
Typing Grades	92.0
Specialist Grades	
Legal Class	15.9
Medical Officer Class	10.1
Professor of Technology	0.5
Scientist Officer	31.8
Higher Scientist Officer	17.8

Table I

Industrial Staff	Percentage who are women
Agric., Food, Fish	42
Courts Service	45
Customs and Excise	27
Defence	33
Employment	59
Environment and Property Service Agency	28
FCO	30
DHSS	60
HO	22
Industry	43
Inland Revenue	54

National Savings	67
Scottish Office	35
Trade (Dept of)	40
Other Depts	43

Table K

Industrial Staff	Percentage who are women
Civil Service Dept Catering	93
Defence	17
Environmental Industry	3
HMSO	19
HO	22
Other Depts	12
All Depts	16

Highest Number of Women in Top Jobs in the Civil Service Depts

DES	97 ⎫ *
HO	67 ⎬
DHSS	58 ⎭
Dept of Environment	33
Dept of Prices and Consumer Protection	28
Royal Households	27
Scottish Office and Scottish Education Dept	25
Libraries, Museums and Galleries	24
FCO	20
Office of Fair Trading	20
Treasury	17
Dept of Trade	16
Councils and Other Organizations	14
Rest Under	10

Dept of Employment	⎫
Board of Inland Revenue	⎬ 8
Ministry of Agriculture, Fisheries and Food	⎫
Land Registry	⎬ 7
N. Ireland Office	⎫
Crown Estate Commissioners	⎪
Dept of Energy	⎬ 6
Dept of Industry	⎭

*Largest Departments in the Civil Service

| Ministry of Overseas Development | |
| Wales Office | 4 |

| Law Chancellors Dept | |
| Law Office and Attorneys General Chambers | 3 |

Central Office of Information	
Office of Fair Trading	2
Law Commission	

Exports, Credits Guarantee Dept	
Dept of National Savings	1
Ordnance Survey	

No Women in Following Depts

Register of Friendly Societies and Office of Independent
  Assurance Officer
Govt Actuary's Dept
Superannuation and Research
Supervision on Independent Companies and Friendly
  Societies
Social Security
Govt Hospitality Fund
Intervention Board for Agricultural Produce
National Dept
National Savings Bank
Saving Certificates, Save-As-You-Earn
Bonds Stocks Office and National Savings Committee
Paymasters' General Office
Privy Council
Public Work Loan Office
Public Prosecution
Royal Mint and Public Record Office

Conclusion

Although these statistics make such gloomy reading, there are a few bright spots on the horizon.

As more and more women go out to work, so employers will come increasingly under pressure to give them more responsibility and more money.

The climate of opinion is changing. Women are beginning to gain confidence in themselves and become less willing to accept second best.

It's up to women themselves to take advantage of these favourable circumstances and strike while the iron is hot.

To misquote Shakespeare, 'There is a tide in the affairs of women, which, taken at the flood, leads on to fortune.'

There have definitely been tides, and in the past they have been linked to wars. During wars, all talk about women not being up to various jobs is forgotten. Women take over practically every 'masculine' job in sight, the government rushes to provide day-nurseries and women are seen running businesses, managing factories, driving trucks, humping coal, ferrying planes and doing all the work which is normally considered far too taxing for such delicate, scatter-brained creatures.

Once the war is over, the men come back, the nurseries are closed, and women are pushed back into their traditional roles of wives, mothers and helpmeets.

During the late forties and early fifties, the pattern was repeated. Women became oppressively 'feminine' and all the old-fashioned 'female' qualities were back in fashion. With the 'New Look', women were beflounced, corseted, put into stiletto heels and winkle-pickers and encouraged to be the helpless, decorative sex-objects which men were apparently in need of at the time.

But official wars, in the traditional sense, are no longer possible. It's all electronics from now on; World War III will be computerized. There are no more epic battles where a man can prove his courage, no more large-scale confrontations, no more glory – tank warfare and aerial dogfights are rapidly going out of style.

War will continue to be with us, but it will be of a different kind because a large-scale, official nuclear war is, one hopes, ruled out. Guerrilla war and street fighting are back in fashion; we are back to tribal warfare.

What has all this got to do with the position of women? Quite a lot, because in traditional wars, all the men went away 'to the front', and it was when they came back to find that women were running things that reaction set in.

Now that men do not periodically have to leave home in large numbers, the pattern has been broken.

Now is the time. Attitudes are changing, and it's up to women themselves to grasp their chances and take the initiative.

Index